PURE ★ GRIT

HOW AMERICAN WORLD WAR II NURSES SURVIVED BATTLE AND PRISON CAMP IN THE PACIFIC

MARY CRONK FARRELL

FOREWORD BY FIRST LIEUTENANT DIANE CARLSON EVANS

Abrams Books for Young Readers • New York

FOR GABE DORAN
AND CHERYL, A WOMAN WITH PURE GRIT

Library of Congress Cataloging-in-Publication Data

Farrell, Mary Cronk.
Pure grit : how American World War II nurses survived battle and prison camp in the Pacific / by Mary Cronk Farrell.
pages cm
Includes bibliographical references and index.
ISBN 978-1-4197-1028-5 (hardcover : alk. paper)
1. Nurses—United States—History—20th century. 2. Military nursing—United States—History—Juvenile literature.
3. World War, 1939–1945—Medical care—United States. 4. World War, 1939–1945—Prisoners and prisons, Japanese—
Juvenile literature. 5. World War, 1939–1945—Campaigns—Philippines—Juvenile literature. 6. Prisoners of war—
United States—Juvenile literature. 7. Prisoners of war—Philippines—Juvenile literature. I. Title.
D807.U6F37 2014
940.54'7573—dc23
2013017134

Text copyright © 2014 Mary Cronk Farrell
Foreword copyright © 2014 Diane Carlson Evans
For image credits, see page 151.
Maps on pages 7 and 9 copyright © 2014 Laura Condouris
Book design by Maria T. Middleton

Printed and bound in China
10 9 8 7 6 5 4 3 2 1

Abrams Books for Young Readers are available at special discounts when purchased in quantity for premiums and
promotions as well as fundraising or educational use. Special editions can also be created to specification. For details,
contact specialsales@abramsbooks.com or the address below.

ABRAMS
THE ART OF BOOKS SINCE 1949

115 West 18th Street
New York, NY 10011
www.abramsbooks.com

CONTENTS

FOREWORD

WHILE SERVING AS AN ARMY NURSE IN THE RICE paddies and jungles of Vietnam in 1968 and '69, I didn't consider the possibility of becoming a prisoner of war. I was twenty-two years old, and my high school and college education had starkly omitted the stories of the Army and Navy nurses held prisoner during World War II in a camp in the Philippines. Nor did I know that during that war, over five hundred American women died in the line of duty, more than two hundred of them Army and Navy nurses. I remember studying Florence Nightingale, who founded modern nursing during the Crimean War, and learning of Clara Barton's heroic role in the Civil War while founding the American Red Cross. But more recent role models and examples were not offered.

War is hell for men. We've always known that. As you read this book, you will discover that war is hell for women, too. When World War II broke out, tens of thousands of women seized the opportunity to serve their country in the military. No law has ever been passed for the conscripting, or drafting, of women into the armed forces. Women were not forced into the ordeal of war, yet they wanted to do the right thing and, without regard for personal safety,

volunteered for duty. This book wonderfully conveys the contribution of women who faced the heartbreak of war by nursing the wounded and dying. These were daring women, shining beacons for those of us who came after them.

During the Vietnam War, unlike any other war in our history, journalists were given unparalleled access. I knew my parents would be watching the 6:00 news showing body bags or dead or bleeding civilians, helicopters crashing into the jungle, napalm and white phosphorus burning villages, and Vietnamese men, women, and children running from the flames. But what they did not see were the nurses in helmets and flak jackets running to the hospitals and treating the men whose torsos and limbs had been ripped open by high-velocity weapons. They did not hear the sound of mortar thuds and rockets piercing our billets and hospital roofs and walls or see us throwing mattresses on top of patients to protect them from shrapnel. They did not see us hanging blood bags, suctioning tracheotomies, and frantically evacuating patients from the hospital to allow more room for mass casualties. In following the footsteps of all military nurses before us, we did the best we could on the battlefield, sharing the tragedy of the spilled blood of our brother soldiers. Reading the heroic stories in this book of the Army and Navy nurses working in the Philippines brought back painful shared memories—of my own time on the battlefield and how much we cared, how we moved beyond our own suffering, and how skilled we became in our work to save lives.

The grim realities of women's service in military nursing, with its hardships and perils, have been underrepresented or lost in the annals of history. Too often eclipsed from the public memory of war and hidden behind cameras, behind male images of war, invisible to our nation at large, are the military women. This gap in our knowledge can be filled, but not so easily now that thousands of the veterans have already passed on, their stories buried with them.

With two memorials in Washington, D.C., now honoring military women—the Vietnam Women's Memorial at the Vietnam Veterans Memorial, and the Women in Military Service to America Memorial, which honors all military women, past, present, and future—their service is now honored and their visibility heightened.

Wars have a face, and until now, with our modern integrated military, that face was masculine. War stories favored those men on the front lines or behind the scenes who were directing the war. In any war, however, the distinction between combatants and noncombatants is meaningless, for both groups are rocketed, machine-gunned, bombed, taken prisoner, and killed. Since women by tradition were not supposed to be in those dangerous situations while in service to their country, historians had largely ignored or purified the experience of military women in the Nurse Corps.

You are about to read an unpurified war story of shared sacrifice among ordinary women caught up in the horrors of close-quarters combat, while doing their best to perform their duty of caring for the wounded. With vivid detail, Mary Cronk Farrell puts a feminine face on warfare. I loved reading about these ordinary women who became extraordinary from the stark terror of the ravages of war. These women were not called warriors or soldiers. But in today's definition, they were warriors and soldiers in every sense.

These women have all passed now. We will never fully know their personal agonies of perpetual fear and living under the hateful eyes of the enemy without comforts of any kind. They endured the trauma of watching young men perish and left a lasting impression on all those thousands of souls they touched. They themselves tried to forget the worst of it.

Reading their stories enriched my life, and I hope it will do the same for you. This book comes close to telling it all. It honors these courageous women and memorializes their mercy, kindness, compassion, and strength of spirit. It captures the pure grit of the finest soldier and the best of humanity.

FIRST LIEUTENANT DIANE CARLSON EVANS, RN, CPT, USA

Army Nurse Corps, 1966-1972
Vietnam, 1968-1969
Founder and President, Vietnam Women's
 Memorial Foundation

5

INTRODUCTION

THE SEEDS OF THIS STORY LAY DORMANT FOR six months in my in-box—one of those e-mails I never found time to read. How was I to know that a paper my cousin wrote for nursing school would change my life forever?

The paper mentioned seventy-nine American military nurses captured by the Japanese in World War II. Astounding! Why hadn't I learned about these women in school? I started research on the prisoner-of-war (POW) nurses that very day.

American women today routinely shipped out to war zones in Iraq and Afghanistan. But the Army and Navy nurses in the Philippines in 1941 never expected to see battle. They learned nursing under fire when the Japanese attacked the Philippines shortly after bombing Pearl Harbor. They treated thousands of wounded soldiers and civilians in jerry-rigged jungle hospitals. When forced to surrender, they stuck together and continued to nurse the sick, the wounded, and the dying. The courage and strength of these women kept them alive through three years of isolation, disease, and starvation. How did they do it? This question impelled my research. The answers became this book.

When I started writing this story, only one of the POW nurses remained alive, Mildred Dalton Manning. Interviewing Millie, along with the sons and daughters of a number of other nurses, brought this story alive for me in a way that the facts and photos could not. The week I polished the final draft, I was greatly saddened to receive the news that Millie had died. She was ninety-nine. The pure grit of Millie and her sister POW nurses has inspired me to act with more courage and resilience in my own life.

American nurses were deployed to the Philippines in the 1930s and '40s to staff hospitals at American Army forts, airfields, and a Navy base. The U.S. military established a presence there at the end of the Spanish-American War in 1898, when the Philippines became a U.S. territory. The islands provided a strategic foothold in East Asia to protect U.S. interests. Of particular value was Manila Bay. It was one of the finest deepwater harbors in the South Pacific and lay protected by the Bataan Peninsula.

As early as 1903, U.S. Army and Navy "brass" had rolled up their sleeves and developed war plans in case of a conflict with Japan.

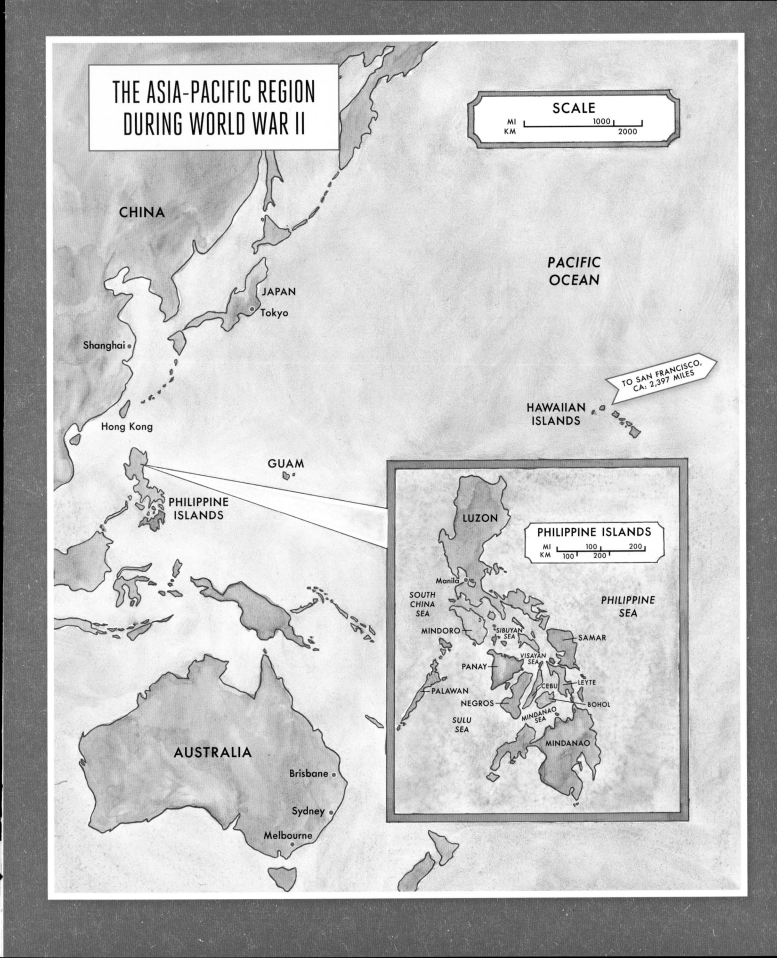

U.S. defense strategists continued to update these plans over the next twenty years. As Japan modernized its weapons and military tactics, forging the Imperial Army and Navy into a swift, ruthless machine, the plan came to be called War Plan Orange (WPO).

When Japan launched a series of invasions in the 1930s and took over Korea, Manchuria, and parts of Russia and China, high-level U.S. military men studied every imaginable scenario of war with Japan, including a sneak air attack on Pearl Harbor and a surprise naval strike on Manila Harbor. In any case, they concluded that a long, costly war would be required to defeat Japan and that the Philippines would be an early casualty in such a conflict.

During the 1920s and '30s the American people had no interest in fighting a war of any kind, having just waged a massive conflict in Europe (World War I, 1914–1918). Neither could the country sustain wartime spending. In the 1920s the U.S. had slashed its military budget for manpower and production, and the Great (economic) Depression in the 1930s necessitated further budget cuts.

American military leaders, though, continued to worry about defense of the Philippines. In 1941 they completed one last war-plan revision, WPO-3. It concentrated a joint Filipino-American Army on Luzon, the largest of the islands. The U.S. War Department sent General Douglas MacArthur to Manila to train and command the newly named U.S. Army Forces in the Far East.

WPO-3 directed MacArthur to protect Manila Bay, and if that failed, withdraw his forces to the Bataan Peninsula and hold out until reinforcements arrived. Most U.S. Navy ships would remain docked on America's West Coast or Hawaii, from which they would be deployed if Japan attacked the Philippines. WPO-3 said nothing about what would happen if defenses on Luzon crumbled before U.S. reinforcements arrived. It made no provision for backing up or rescuing American soldiers in the Philippines. It made no mention of Army or Navy nurses.

This plan was known only to a select group in the War Department and President Franklin Roosevelt. Military nurses knew nothing of WPO-3, but in 1941 there were signs of trouble. That spring the Army and Navy evacuated all families of personnel in the Philippines. The number of ships arriving in Manila with fighting men and military supplies more than tripled, and twice the number of Army nurses debarked, some coming on transports carrying tanks in the holds. In July MacArthur started to beef up training of Filipino soldiers. He believed that the Japanese might attack the islands as early as that coming April.

But this is not the story of generals, soldiers, or military strategists. This is the story of American military women serving in the Philippines when the Japanese attacked the islands on December 8, 1941. This is the story of the first large group of American women sent into combat and how they rose to the duty to which they were called.

LUZON ISLAND, PHILIPPINES, DURING WORLD WAR II

LUZON

LINGAYEN GULF

• Baguio

POW CAMP CABANATUAN

CLARK FIELD

POW CAMP O'DONNELL

• San Fernando

FORT STOTSENBURG

HOSPITAL NO. 1 1ST SITE

BATAAN

HOSPITAL NO. 1 2ND SITE

Limay

HOSPITAL NO. 2

Mariveles

Manila

CORREGIDOR (MALINTA TUNNEL)

CAVITE NAVAL SHIPYARD

LAGUNA DE BAY

• Los Baños

PHILIPPINE SEA

MARINDUQUE

MINDORO

Manila inset

Manila

SANTO TOMAS UNIVERSITY

BILIBID PRISON

PASIG RIVER

ARMY-NAVY CLUB

STERNBERG HOSPITAL

MANILA BAY

CAÑACAO NAVAL HOSPITAL

CAVITE NAVAL SHIPYARD

FORT MCKINLEY

NICHOLS FIELD

SCALE
MI   2   4
KM 2   4

SCALE
MI   25   50
KM   50

CHAPTER 1
ADVENTURE AND ROMANCE

JULY 1940
Manila, Philippine Islands

Ethel Thor stood breathless at the rail of the USS *U. S. Grant* sailing into Manila Bay. The ship slipped past Corregidor Island, revealing great battleships and tiny fishing boats anchored in the harbor. Brilliant blue sky reflected in the deep water. Rugged purple peaks rose to the north. Lush jungle sprawled over the hills and down to the shell-white sand and the lapping surf.

A tall redhead with hazel eyes, Ethel had grown up an orphan in Tacoma, Washington, living with an older sister after her parents died. Quiet, well liked, and hardworking, she had a streak of independence that led her to join the U.S. Army Nurse Corps (ANC). Her voyage on the military troopship had taken twenty-eight long days across the Pacific. Now here she was—one of six women on a boatload of soldiers eight thousand miles from home— about to go ashore in the Philippine Islands, a tropical wonderland.

Ethel's dress clung to her skin in the tropical heat. She wrinkled her nose at the smell of seaweed and dead fish but gazed in wonder at the city. Grand homes encircled Manila's harbor. Coconut palms swayed along shoreline avenues and shaded the grand Manila Hotel. Cathedral spires and Fort Santiago rose from Manila's colonial walled city.

While Ethel cruised into Manila Bay in July 1940, much of the world roiled with conflict. Germany had crushed most of Europe by using a new war tactic called blitzkrieg, where troops, tanks, and airplanes all attacked at once. Now Nazi leader Adolf Hitler prepared to blitzkrieg England. In the Far East, Japan was on the march. The previous month Britain had ordered the evacuation of all British women and children from Hong Kong, fearing Japan would capture the city. The only democratic powers left in the world were the United States and Great Britain.

But war seemed far away to Ethel Thor as the *U. S. Grant* powered toward Manila's piers. A crowd waved from the dock. An Army band in white uniforms struck up a lively tune with their shining brass instruments. Ethel and five other Army nurses went ashore dressed in heels, nylon stockings, and gloves. Greeted by their new leader, Miss E. Valine Messner, the chief nurse of the Philippine Command, they were given corsages in a brief welcoming ceremony.

The next day, Ethel reported for duty as a scrub nurse in the operating room at the U.S. Army Sternberg General Hospital in downtown Manila. She slipped easily into the routine of surgical cases—mostly officers' kids having tonsils or appendixes out, or wives in childbirth. Except for one area set aside for Filipinos, medical cases at the 450-bed hospital were U.S. military personnel or their dependents. The hospital also served retired U.S. military personnel and their families who lived in the Philippines, but aside from contracting the occasional tropical fever or parasite, military families were young and healthy.

Duty was light compared to the twelve-hour shifts Ethel had worked in civilian hos-

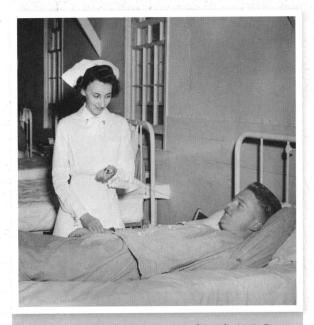

Opposite: **Nurses arriving in Manila, July 1941. Front row, left to right: Mr. Anderson, Madeline Ullom, Lieutenant Seamon, Captain Cotter, and Ethel Thor. Back row: Juanita Redmond, Sue Downing, Adele Foreman, Clara Mueller.**

Above: **A U.S. Army nurse attending a patient, Camp Forrest training base in Tullahoma, Tennessee, 1941.**

pitals and at her prior station at Letterman Army Hospital in San Francisco. Since the hot, humid weather could be tiring for people from the States, nurses worked only four hours on the day shifts. They rotated through eight-hour shifts in the cooler temperatures overnight.

The women enjoyed a casual, resort-like atmosphere in their quarters at the rear of the hospital. Mahogany fans cooled the rooms, drawing the fragrance of gardenias in through the open windows. Outside, purple bougainvillea and yellow plumeria bloomed. Orchids grew everywhere, like dandelions in Ethel's home state of Washington. Hired Filipinos did the laundry, cooking, and cleaning. A servant often served meals.

The only dilemma facing Ethel and the other young nurses was choosing free-time activities. Go to the beach? Visit peaceful palm groves or mountain forests? Take in the fascinating Philippine culture? Many learned to play golf, tennis, or badminton. In the heat of the day there was bowling, movies, or shopping. And, of course, there were scores of young American men—Navy sailors in white tunics and trousers, and Army soldiers, stand-up-straight spiffy in their khakis.

The sailors came into Manila on leave from Cavite Naval Shipyard, visible a short distance across the water on Cavite Peninsula. The soldiers hailed from four nearby Army posts—Fort William McKinley, seven miles south of Manila; Fort Stotsenberg, adjoined by Clark Field roughly seventy miles north of the city; Fort Mills on Corregidor Island, a short boat trip across the harbor; and Camp John Hay in the cool, pine-scented northern mountains near the village of Baguio.

Military nurses lived and worked at each site.

Ethel discovered that American women were popular at the Manila Army-Navy OC (Officers' Club). They could walk the short distance from Sternberg, beat the heat with a dip in the pool, or relax on the veranda and sip icy drinks. Uncle Sam provided plenty of partners for dinner and dancing. The young women talked and laughed while the sun set and danced while the moon rose.

"Each evening we dressed for dinner in long dresses. The men dressed in tuxedos, dinner jackets with the cummerbunds," said Army Nurse Earlyn "Blackie" Black, stationed at Fort Mills on Corregidor. "It was a very formal type of living. Even to go to the movies, we'd put on long dresses."

Ethel had dropped out of high school at seventeen and moved into St. Joseph's Hospital and School of Nursing in Tacoma. Nursing students worked long hours for low pay, but upon graduation they could earn enough to

Ethel Thor (in white skirt) takes friends on a picnic and a drive to the famous bat cave at Montalban Gorge, Luzon. From left: Army nurses Frances Nash (sitting), Ruby Motely, Ida Pecshon, and Clara Mueller. January 1941.

U.S. Navy men relax and dance with their dates in a hotel ballroom shortly before the Japanese attack on the Philippines. Manila, November 1941.

support themselves. That appealed to Ethel. Her quiet, capable manner and caring instincts made nursing a good fit for her.

During the Great Depression, Ethel worked as a nurse for the Civilian Conservation Corps at Fort Lewis, near Tacoma. When one of the Army doctors suggested she join the Army Nurse Corps, it seemed a no-brainer—a guaranteed job with good pay. She went back to school at night to earn her high school diploma, then enlisted in the ANC in 1938.

JULY–NOVEMBER 1941

A YEAR AFTER ETHEL ARRIVED IN THE PHILIPpines, U.S. Army brass named General Douglas MacArthur to lead a newly formed command in the Philippines. Filipino-American forces included U.S. Army troops, thirty-one thousand strong, and one hundred and twenty thousand Philippine men. Ethel didn't know that MacArthur expected Japan to attack the Philippines. She didn't know Japan was churning out Mitsubishi Zero fighter

LIEUT. H. B. BRANTLEY
A.N.C.   78 B

LIEUT. EARLEEN ALLEN
A.N.C.   78 B

LIEUT. F. A. FELLMETH
A.N.C.   78 B

LIEUT. M. J. OBERST

planes—faster, more maneuverable, and with bigger guns than any planes Americans had ever seen.

That summer and fall, the number of troopships arriving in Manila carrying U.S. soldiers, military equipment, and nurses more than tripled. Thirty more Army nurses came, including Mildred "Millie" Dalton from Georgia. She was one of eighty-eight Army nurses now stationed on Luzon. Like the others, she wore a white dress and cap for work, the same as her former civilian uniform except for the small military badge on the collar. Her duties in the peacetime service remained similar to the work she'd done in civilian life. U.S. military nurses had only relative rank, which meant they had no military title but were addressed as "Miss." Nothing in her training had readied her to work in a war zone.

"There was no way in the world we were prepared for war," Millie said, "or even told anything about being prepared for war."

U.S. NAVY NURSES ALSO ARRIVED IN MANILA that fall.

Nurse Margaret Nash had supervised surgery for two years in the U.S. Naval Hospital on the Pacific island of Guam. Margaret—Peggy, to her friends—was making plans to leave the Navy. She'd fallen in love with a naval officer, and military nurses could not be married.

"Ed was the executive officer on the USS *Penguin.* We went together for about seven months and got engaged to be married. And from then on our lives were just a ball."

Peggy had long showed a spirit of adventure. Few girls where she grew up near Wilkes-Barre, Pennsylvania, would have finished nursing school and gone on to graduate work. Fewer still would have volunteered on a Coast Guard cutter during the St. Patrick's Day Flood of '36, the worst flood of the Susquehanna River Valley in known history. Peggy's uncle, a congressman surveying the rising waters, ran into her one day.

"What are your plans?" he asked.

"I don't know," Peggy answered.

"How would you like to join the Navy?" her uncle asked.

Peggy didn't hesitate. "Sure, I'd love it, but don't tell my mother."

Several years after joining the U.S. Navy Nurse Corps, Peggy got orders to the Guam Naval Hospital. One day in October 1941, the chief nurse interrupted Peggy in surgery. "You'd better let your senior nurse take over. Your orders are in," she said.

"Well, why don't we finish this operation?" Peggy asked.

"You don't have time," the chief nurse told her. "You have to be aboard ship in two hours. . . . You are being transferred to Manila."

Shocked, Peggy went to pack. It was her first inkling of trouble.

AS PEGGY NASH SAILED FOR MANILA, ARMY Nurse Rita Palmer left San Francisco, also headed for the Philippines. Rita reported to Fort Stotsenberg Station Hospital, roughly seventy miles north of Manila. For twenty-two-year-old Rita, the perks at Stotsenberg came dressed in standard-issue leather bomber jackets. These daring young pilots flew the new B-17 Flying Fortress bombers at nearby Clark Field. Many were handsome, single, and more than happy to see a girl from the States. Not to be outdone, soldiers from the fort's tank battalion took nurses for a ride in their armored vehicle. They were proud of their tank, like boys playing with a new toy.

Navy Nurse Peggy Nash, c. 1941.

"We were in a strange and different country. We were excited by everything we did," Rita said. "I remember being told by pilots that they were flying into formations of Japanese planes, and they were concerned. But I don't think . . . we gave it a second thought."

AS RITA SETTLED IN AT FORT STOTSENBERG, Peggy Nash arrived at Cañacao Naval Hospital, roughly twenty miles south of Manila. The hospital served the Cavite Naval Shipyard, visible a short distance across Cañacao Bay on the Cavite Peninsula, about a half-mile walk by land. Peggy was one of twelve Navy nurses on duty there.

In March, six months before, the Navy had evacuated all military wives and children from the Philippines. Navy nurses at Cañacao had been advised to send home any valuables.

They practiced blackouts in case of nighttime air raids, and nurses were told to order supplies they needed to ready their wards for casualties. They made and sterilized hundreds of surgical dressings, equipped their wards with plasma, saline solution, IV equipment, suture material, adhesive, bandages, bandage scissors, and extra blankets.

But Peggy had just arrived. She hadn't been part of these preparations at Cañacao. The first week of December, she went into Manila to make arrangements with a priest for her wedding. She and Ed had decided to marry on Valentine's Day. The Navy discharged women who married, and Ed's tour was almost done. She missed him terribly, but the USS *Penguin* would arrive soon.

"I had no idea there was going to be a war," said Peggy. "That's how naive I was."

CHAPTER 2
SURPRISE ATTACK

DECEMBER 8, 1941 + DAY ONE
Luzon, Philippine Islands

Hours before daylight, Navy nurses at Cañacao Naval Hospital woke to pounding on their doors.

"Wake up! No, don't turn your light on! It's a blackout," called the nurse who ran from room to room, telling the women to get dressed and get downstairs.

"A drill at this hour?"

"Hell, no! The Japanese are bombing Pearl Harbor!"

The Philippines lie on the other side of the international date line from Hawaii, so while the attack on Pearl Harbor occurred at 7:55 Sunday morning, December 7, in Manila it was early morning Monday, December 8.

The first person in the Philippines to hear of the Japanese attack was a U.S. Navy radioman who caught something on the airwaves at about 2:30 A.M. He called a friend at the Cañacao nurses' quarters after notifying his commanding officer.

Navy nurses gathered downstairs to receive their orders: discharge to active duty any naval officer or sailor who could walk. The women rushed out into the dawn. Dodging mud puddles left from recent rains, they ran more than a block to the hospital.

ONE HUNDRED AND FIFTY MILES NORTH, HIGH in the mountains near the village of Baguio, Army Nurse Ruby Bradley was on duty that morning at the Camp John Hay hospital, sterilizing instruments for a routine surgery. The surgeon summoned Ruby and told her not to bother gloving and gowning for the operation—the Japanese had attacked Pearl Harbor.

Just then, an explosion sounded outside, so loud, Ruby's ears rang. Running to the window, she saw bombs falling, the Japanese planes coming in so low, she saw the pilots' faces!

The Japanese dropped fifty bombs. None hit the hospital, but casualties quickly rolled in.

"There were thirty-seven that came in right away. There were about as many killed as alive," Ruby said. "We were lucky, though, because if this had happened just five minutes later, when the troops are out on the field in the morning, we would have had many more casualties."

AT ABOUT THIS TIME, ETHEL THOR AND OTHER nurses at Sternberg Hospital in Manila heard about the attack on Pearl Harbor. The news traveled fast. Details sketchy. Impossible to believe. Tears flowed as word came of heavy American casualties. Many nurses had friends stationed in Hawaii.

"Girls! Girls!" Chief Nurse Josephine "Josie" Nesbit shouted to nurses going off night shift.

"You've got to sleep today. You can't weep and wail over this, because you have to work tonight."

Nurses did not yet know of the attack on Camp John Hay, but if war had truly started, they suspected that the Japanese would target the Philippines next. Nurses winced when handed twenty-year-old gas masks and helmets, equipment from the Great War. But they tried them on and studied pamphlets telling how to detect poisonous gases and care for gassed patients.

Then supervisors told nurses to go about their regular routine. The danger seemed so unreal at Fort McKinley that Army nurses Hattie Brantley and Minnie Breese took the masks and kept their tee time at the golf course.

U.S. Army nurses in the Philippines were issued gas masks in May 1941. Here, nurses test them two weeks before the Japanese attack.

A Vought O2U floatplane flies over Cavite Naval Shipyard, c. 1936. Cañacao Naval Hospital, part of Sangley Point Naval Station, is in the background, in front of the left two radio towers.

BACK AT CAÑACAO NAVAL HOSPITAL, CONFU-sion reigned as Peggy Nash and the entire staff rallied. By 10:30 A.M. all able-bodied patients had their discharge orders so they could report to their stations. Rumors circulated that the Japanese had bombed the coast of California. Nurses worried that nearby Cavite Naval Ship-yard would be targeted.

At noon Peggy and the others sat down for lunch. Before they'd taken a bite, the air-raid siren wailed. Nurses gaped at one another, wondering where to run, where to hide, finally fleeing to the crawl space under the building to sit in the dirt.

Soon the all-clear sounded. No bombs had fallen, the only casualty their once-white uni-forms. Headquarters sent boxes of sailors' jeans and work shirts, but the low-slung bell-bottoms were not designed to fit women. As nurses tried them on, the room filled with gales of laughter.

"I'll die before I wear these," Peggy said.

While they were laughing, bombs dropped on Clark Field at Fort Stotsenberg.

Fort Stotsenberg Station Hospital

AS AT CAÑACAO, RITA PALMER AND THE OTHER nurses at Stotsenberg had been ordered to discharge all able-bodied men from the hospi-tal. Everyone talked about Pearl Harbor, but nobody at Stotsenberg or Clark Field knew the severity of the attack—the Pacific Fleet had been destroyed, snuffing out any chance of its aiding the Philippines.

Nine hours after the bombing of Pearl Harbor, Rita was eating lunch when the shriek of air-raid sirens ripped the air. Seconds later, bombs whistled down and hit with deafening explosions. She sprinted to the hospital, the ground rolling with shock waves.

Bombs dropped in droves from planes painted with the red rising sun of the Japanese Empire. The bull's-eye of their target was Clark Field, two blocks away.

Pilots raced for their planes. Soldiers ran to their antiaircraft guns. No air-raid shelters had been built, no trenches dug. Some men dove into drainage ditches, shooting their rifles at the Japanese bombers—bombers flying thousands of feet beyond the reach of American antiaircraft artillery.

The eastern sky turned black with smoke. From the hospital windows, Rita watched as fire blazed from barracks and hangars. American B-17 bombers and P-40 fighters lined up on the tarmac burst into fireballs, igniting grass and trees surrounding the airfield. Three P-40 fighters rose from the inferno, only to be shot from the sky.

Nurses barely comprehended the bombings before waves of Japanese Zero fighters zipped in. Planes darted in and out of the columns of smoke, their machine guns strafing Clark Field—virtually unopposed.

Stotsenberg's few ambulances brought in the first wounded men, jolting Rita and the other nurses into action. The bombardment had spared them, but its aftermath soon filled the hospital with hundreds of wounded and dying men. Rita had no preparation for such slaughter. In fact, the Army nurses had never had any training for combat nursing.

Wards overflowed. The wounded lay on the porches, some on litters, some on the ground. Nurses gave shot after shot of morphine—to deaden the men's pain and quiet their screaming. They sorted the patients into three groups: those whom doctors would need to treat first, those whose wounds did not look fatal, and those they could only make comfortable until they died. The nurses had read about working triage in textbooks but had never expected to make these grave choices themselves.

Rita had no time for feelings. She hadn't even time to keep charts. Nurses put signs on the foreheads of some of the badly wounded, listing the drugs and dosage they'd been given. A patient called one nurse's name, but his face was so badly burned, she couldn't recognize him. The women labored nonstop—stanching blood, bandaging wounds, easing agony if possible. One soldier's blood soaked through his mattress. Another victim embodied Rita's horror: a sixteen-year-old boy who had lied about his age to get into the Army lost both his legs.

Many of the men had taken cover facedown on the ground. Bomb concussions and strafing bullets had driven dirt and debris into their faces. Nurses did what they could to clean and soothe damaged skin and blinded eyes with bath towels soaked in cool water. The worst of these cases had also had their backsides blown away, muscles and tissue ripped off, leaving huge wounds that would require months to heal.

By midafternoon the number of wounded overwhelmed the Stotsenberg doctors and nurses. The medical staff called Sternberg Hospital in Manila, pleading for help. Afternoon turned to evening without a break for Rita or the others. Finally, close to midnight, help came: five Army nurses, four doctors, and fifteen Filipino nurses.

Swamped with such suffering, the nurses grasped at anything to stay sane and keep going. Surgical teams released tension with black humor. The absurdity of one Army nurse having brought her golf clubs from Manila in hopes of having time to visit the country club lent comic relief as they operated through the night and next day.

In the days that followed, nurses dressed wounds, gave shots for pain relief, and tried to make dying men comfortable. It became routine, though it was anything but. The beauty and peace of Fort Stotsenberg and Clark Field had vanished. The Japanese attack had killed 85 men, wounded 350, and demolished nearly half the strength of America's Far East Air Force. For the first time, nurses at Stotsenberg were issued dog tags—a means of identification in case of death.

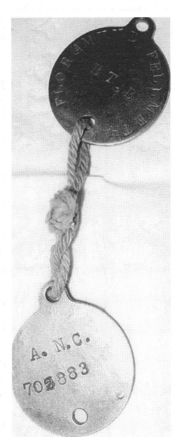

Opposite: U.S. B-17 bombers and P-40 fighters on the Clark Field runway under Japanese attack. North of Manila, December 8, 1941.

Left: Army Nurse Floramund Fellmeth used a hammer and letter and number punches to pound her name and serial number into these metal discs. These served as her identification throughout the war.

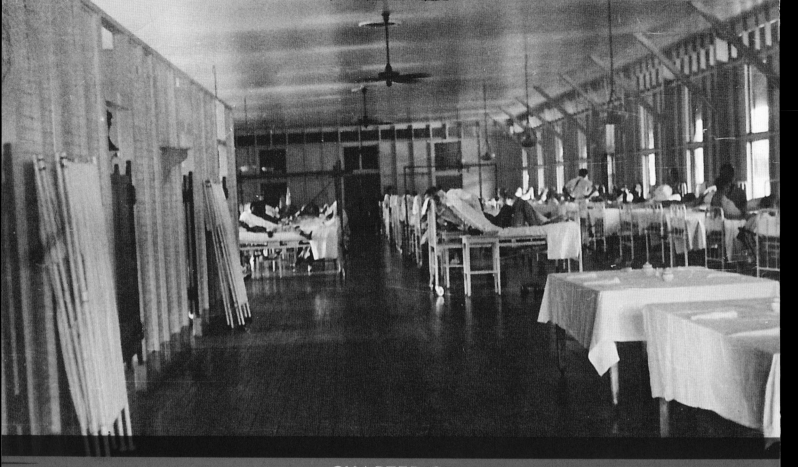

CHAPTER 3
NO TIME FOR FEAR

Sternberg, the largest and best-equipped medical facility in the Philippines, became the center for military and civilian casualties.

"Girls, we're at war," the hospital commander told Sternberg's nurses. "Each of us has a job to do. I'm sure you'll do yours well."

A deluge of wounded soldiers and airmen arrived by ambulance and train from Forts Stotsenberg and McKinley. "I often slept on the operating room table," said Army Nurse Madeline Ullom, "or put a little pad in the corner, someplace to go to sleep."

Of all the Army nurses at Sternberg, Frances Nash (no relation to Peggy Nash) may have been the best prepared for combat duty. The gutsy Georgia farm girl had made up her mind to become a nurse and applied to nursing school as a teenager. Frances learned life-and-death nursing in the emergency room of Grady Memorial Hospital in Atlanta, one of the largest public hospitals in the country.

22

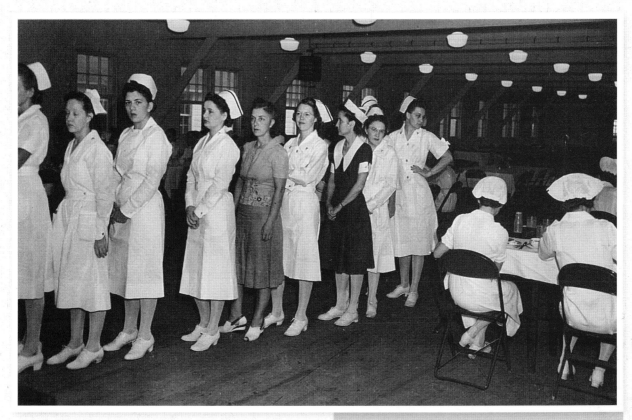

Most Americans in the 1930s believed nursing was not a proper place for innocent girls fresh out of high school. Some mothers felt shamed by their daughters' nursing duties, which included exposure to naked men, emptying bedpans, and doing "other disgusting things for people." Virtuous unmarried women were expected to remain ignorant of male anatomy and the nature of sexual relations. Knowledge itself was deemed proof of impurity.

Still, despite the risk to their reputations, the hard work, and pay as low as sixteen cents an hour, girls like Frances swarmed to nursing schools. For those who couldn't afford college, nursing school provided job skills and income during the Great Depression.

Grueling years of patient care earned Frances her cap and pin in 1932. She worked in Grady's emergency room and surgery until she joined the Army Nurse Corps in 1935. Arriving in Manila in 1940, Frances was confident and outgoing, a popular face at Sternberg Hospital, where she worked with Ethel Thor.

And yet the seemingly unending stream of wounded men coming into surgery devastated Frances. She and her cohort kept going by riveting their attention on their patients. One nurse, her eyes red and swollen, worked on after receiving the news that her boyfriend had become an early casualty of war. Another got news that her fiancé had died of a head wound in the hospital at Fort Stotsenberg. Despite their lack of readiness for war, the nurses plunged in with body, mind, and heart.

DECEMBER 10, 1941 + DAY THREE
Cañacao Naval Hospital, near Manila

PEGGY NASH AND THE OTHER NURSES AT Cañacao Naval Hospital braced themselves, wondering if and when they would come under attack. As before, they were at lunch in their quarters near the hospital when the air-raid sirens blew. Peggy and the others carried their food into the crawl space under the building. Balancing plates on their laps, they put up a good front, giggling and trading nervous quips. When the sirens stopped, silence reigned for long minutes. The nurses relaxed, thinking someone had neglected to give the all-clear signal.

Suddenly the roar of planes filled their ears, followed by blasts of bombs exploding. Anti-aircraft guns growled from the nearby navy yard. Peggy shuddered in silence as wave after wave of explosions shook the building above and the ground beneath them.

Several nurses mouthed prayers. One buried her head against her propped-up knees, fingering rosary beads in trembling hands. The bombardment lasted five minutes . . . ten . . . fifteen . . . a timeless monotony of pounding upon pounding.

After forty-five minutes of earsplitting explosions, the silence felt equally deafening. The nurses crept from their hiding place. Half a mile across Cañacao Bay, swelling clouds of smoke darkened the sky. Sporadic flames flared. Cavite Naval Shipyard was demolished.

They ran to the hospital, where casualties streamed in, Navy and civilian. Peggy saw both military and civilian wounded coming four or five in a car, some even on the roof. Patients arrived on splintered doors, dirty carpets, blankets, woven bamboo mats, and twisted corrugated roofing. The entire hospital became an emergency ward, every doctor a surgeon. This left Peggy and the other nurses to administer needed medications without doctors' orders. Scattered two to a ward, they worked in tan-

Opposite: Christmas at the U.S. Army nurses' quarters, Sternberg Hospital, Manila, 1940. Frances Nash is in the second row from the top, on the far right, with Ethel Thor in the row in front of her, also on the far right.

Above: U.S. Cavite Naval Shipyard aflame after a Japanese air attack. Small-arms shells explode (left) and a torpedo-loaded barge (center) burns. December 10, 1941.

dem, one going down a row of wounded with a syringe of tetanus vaccine, the other following with morphine. As they finished with each row of wounded, they started on the next.

The stench of burning flesh nauseated Peggy, as did the sight of mangled bodies—oily, dirty, and bleeding; arms and legs at weird angles, some dangling by a shred, others only jagged stumps. As bodies left for the morgue, corpsmen lifted patients from the floor into beds without changing the linens. It couldn't be helped.

"It was amazing how cool the nurses were. I never thought I could be like that," Peggy said later. "The patients were two or three in a bed, and on chairs between beds. As we readied patients for surgery, sometimes we came to a bed, and the patient was already dead."

"Could I have a glass of water?" a child asked, as Peggy walked by. She promised to bring it. "By the time I got back, he was dead. That just about killed me.

"The next time I looked out the window, it was dark, and there was fire all around, and the sky was red with flames and smoke. Manila was burning.

"I thought to myself, if the Japanese came and dropped another load, this suffering would all be over, mine included."

On an errand to the operating room, Peggy saw doctors operating on every table, on the floor, and even the steps. "It was like a nightmare in there, but I couldn't stop to help because I had to get back to the ward. We worked into the night. Corpses filled the morgue. There was no time for fear."

CHAPTER 4
NURSES UNDER FIRE

DECEMBER 1941
U.S. Army Sternberg General Hospital,
Manila

For the next week, scores of Japanese planes filled the sky over Manila, still bombing Cavite Naval Shipyard, nearby Nichols Field, and Fort McKinley. Nurses learned to expect flights of bombers attacking the nearby city docks each noon, even though the rush of wounded that followed would have been unimaginable to them just days before.

Explosions rocked the hospital building. Chandeliers in its dining room swung, windows shattered, glass sprayed, patients screamed. A bomb concussion knocked down ANC Commander Maude Campbell Davison, injuring her spine. She had only recently taken over the command when Miss Messner rotated back to the States. Now she was a patient.

Only a handful of American planes had survived the assault on Clark Field. From the Sternberg windows Army Nurse Juanita Redmond watched them bravely take on the enemy. "Our planes brought down three of theirs one afternoon."

Nurses were told to go outside during the noontime air raids in case the hospital got a direct hit. Soldiers dug trenches outside the wards, operating rooms, and living quarters. Patients who could walk took safety in the trenches. Nurses moved other patients under their beds for protection and then leaped into the nearest foxhole themselves.

After two weeks of steady bombings, nurses heard the Japanese Imperial Army had sailed into the Lingayen Gulf, 130 miles north of Manila. Seventy-six transports loaded with more than forty-three thousand soldiers dropped anchor the night of December 21. The next morning the well-trained, well-equipped, and battle-experienced Japanese took the beaches.

The nurses did not know that U.S. General Douglas MacArthur had begun training the Philippine Army only six months prior. Most Filipino soldiers had no uniforms, blankets, gas masks, or tools to dig trenches. The Filipinos carried old rifles used by American soldiers in World War I. Many units went into battle without ever having fired their weapons. Big of heart but small in readiness, the troops crumbled and retreated under the massive Japanese assault.

Nurses knew that the Japanese Army was advancing. From the beaches at Lingayen a wide valley formed a natural highway heading straight to Manila. The Filipino-American forces had only one option: fall back to the Bataan Peninsula and fight a delaying action until reinforcements could arrive—War Plan Orange-3.

General MacArthur and his headquarters staff picked up and moved to the fortified island of Corregidor at the mouth of Manila Bay. Top naval officers aboard the two surviving Navy ships lifted anchor and sailed to Australia.

Morale sank at the hospital. Nurses continued to crack jokes to keep up their spirits. When one woman bemoaned her loss of appetite, another quipped that if she were hit by a shell, an empty stomach might improve her chance of survival.

During a bombing raid at Sternberg, Army Nurse Dorothy Scholl stayed with her patients, later seeing the man she'd been dating, Second Lieutenant Harold Armold, and a priest in the nearest foxhole. "I couldn't have gotten in if I had tried," she said, laughing.

AS JAPANESE ATTACKS IN THE SOUTH PACIFIC intensified, American and British leaders met to strategize military tactics in a conflict rapidly spreading around the globe. President Franklin Roosevelt promised to focus most U.S. military resources on the war in Europe. General MacArthur was advised to do the best he could with what he had. U.S. Secretary of War Henry Stimson noted in his diary, *Everybody knows chances are against our getting relief to him, but there is no use saying so beforehand.*

In a strategy to end the bombing and loss of civilian life, General MacArthur declared Manila an "open city." The 1907 Hague Convention rules of war prohibited any military activity in an open city.

Opposite: **Japanese soldiers strategically landed at various points throughout the invasion. Here, they land at Corregidor, on May 4, 1942.**

27

The U.S. withdrawal commenced. Troops marched out. Every barge and boat that could float was loaded with supplies for the Army to defend itself against the Japanese for as long as possible. Within twenty-four hours Corregidor Island was stocked to support ten thousand troops. Every available transport via water, road, and rail was commandeered to supply forces retreating to Bataan. Ammunition had already been stored on the peninsula, as well as petroleum and canned food.

Army nurses from Fort Stotsenberg and Fort McKinley had all evacuated to Sternberg

Army nurses wearing gas masks, c. 1941.

with their patients by December 23. That evening the Sternberg commander interrupted the nurses' supper.

"Girls, pack your white duty uniforms," he told them. "We are going to Bataan tomorrow."

"That's the first time most of us had ever heard of Bataan," said Hattie Brantley, a young nurse from farm country near the town of Jefferson, Texas. As she and her friends prepared to evacuate Manila, their "conferences and arguments about what to take along and what to leave behind were numerous and protracted."

They stuffed underclothing, a few precious possessions, such as photographs and favorite books, and whatever else they could fit into one duffel bag apiece. Rita Palmer packed her black nightie. Another woman fashioned slender pockets inside the pant legs and waist of the extra-large army coveralls she'd been issued. She filled them with tampons.

Ethel "Sally" Blaine, a young nurse who enjoyed looking her best, later realized she'd lost her makeup and nice clothes in the hurried retreat to Bataan. Another left in riding boots and later had no serviceable shoes.

CHRISTMAS EVE 1941

AT 5:30 THE NEXT MORNING, CHRISTMAS EVE day, the first twenty-five Army nurses joined doctors and corpsmen in a convoy of buses and military trucks. Dressed for duty in white uniforms, stockings, and caps, they headed for Bataan, and U.S. Army General Hospital No. 1.

The big yellow public buses driving them

to Bataan had open sides, which proved handy several miles outside of the city when Japanese bombers appeared overhead. The nurses jumped out of the vehicles, diving into ditches along the road. Focused on survival, they had no idea they were making history as the first group of American Army women ordered into combat.

FRANKIE LEWEY, A FEISTY REDHEAD FROM DALhart, Texas, had argued her way into the Army Nurse Corps despite being older than the twenty-eight-year age limit. She left her hometown nursing job, telling her mother, "If ever there is a war, I hope I get right in the thick of it."

Maybe she remembered those words on the bus jolting toward the Bataan Peninsula. As their convoy neared the town of San Fernando, artillery fire sounded to the east. American tanks and troops were fighting to hold back the Japanese, fighting to give the Filipino-American forces time to retreat.

Reaching Layac Junction at the base of the Bataan Peninsula, the convoy turned south, and the day wore on. Temperatures soared over ninety degrees. Native water buffalo, called carabao, wallowed in water holes for relief, and Filipino children ran naked. The buses passed through the swampy area of the Culo River, a hatchery for swarms of mosquitoes carrying malaria.

Top: A Japanese bombardment airplane probably over Luzon, c. 1941.

Bottom: Army Nurse Frankie Lewey before the war.

Still, Frankie and the other nurses felt relieved to escape the bombing. They rattled down East Road, anticipating cool sheets and a good night's sleep. The rocky, one-lane route followed the coast of Bataan and formed the western boundary of Manila Bay. Rice paddies gave way to coconut groves, then to a dense jungle of spreading acacia trees, rampant vines, and thick underbrush.

The steamy, fertile tangle of vegetation could not have been more different from the windy, high plains of the Oklahoma Panhandle where Frankie was born.

Her mother ran a boardinghouse and restaurant in a Texas-Oklahoma border town. Frankie's job as a young girl had been to fill the oil lanterns and clean their glass chimneys. She had liked caring for people but wanted adventure, too. Frankie moved more than halfway across the state of Texas to go to nursing school, and later to Washington, D.C., for psy-chiatric nurse training. Remaining single, gaining higher education, and nursing the mentally ill—all this had strained Frankie's family ties. Some of Frankie's aunts and cousins cut off all contact with her. She entered the Army Nurse Corps in 1940 at Fort Sam Houston, Texas. In the summer of 1941, Frankie was assigned to Fort McKinley, on the outskirts of Manila. In her off-duty hours she volunteered at a nearby leper colony. After the Japanese bombed Fort McKinley in the first week of December, Frankie and the other nurses there moved into the city, where casualties mounted at Stern-berg Hospital.

The sun had set when the buses carrying Frankie Lewey and the other nurses pulled into the sleepy fishing village of Limay, a group of tiny bamboo shacks set high on stilts. Wide-eyed children watched the line of trucks and buses crawling down the dirt road toward the beach and Hospital No. 1.

Right: A water buffalo native to the Philippines, called a carabao, wallows to cool itself.

Opposite: Beds made. Mosquito nets handy. At Hospital No. 1, an Army nurse enjoys a quiet moment before casualties arrive. Bataan, December 1941.

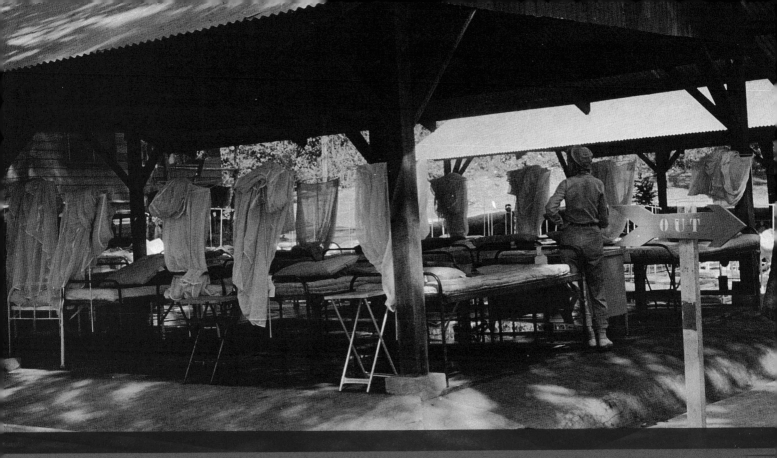

CHAPTER 5
RETREAT TO THE JUNGLE

DECEMBER 1941
U.S. Army General Hospital No. 1,
Limay, Bataan Peninsula

The Army nurses expected to arrive at a hospital. They stared in shock at the former training camp for Filipino troops. As John Glusman states in his book *Conduct Under Fire*, "to call it a hospital was like calling a hut a hotel." Camp Limay was a deserted cluster of sheds with palm-thatch roofs and bamboo shutters held open with sticks. A pipe outside each shed supplied water.

The women carried their belongings off the buses and stretched their tired muscles. Choosing one of the twenty long, narrow barracks for their quarters, they entered to find several small rooms with a few scattered beds.

One small voice asked what they all wanted to know. "Do we sleep on the floor?"

A soldier pointed them to a corrugated-tin warehouse where beds and bedding were stored. The women made numerous trips back and forth, carrying footboards, headboards, mattresses, and linens. They assembled the beds and tucked in the sheets.

Then they walked to the beach, where the mess crew prepared pancakes for supper. They relaxed on the sand to the quiet murmur of waves. The starlit evening was peaceful—unless they looked across the bay, where the U.S. Navy was blowing up ammunition dumps and burning one million gallons of oil to keep them from the Japanese. Flames leapt a hundred feet into the sky over Manila.

The nurses slipped away to bed.

ARMY NURSES CONTINUED TO EVACUATE Manila. Madeline Ullom rode with patients in an ambulance to the wharf, headed for Fort Mills Hospital on Corregidor Island.

"We dodged bomb craters. No car lights, just the light of the stars and the moon. We got on this little inter-island boat." In the gray light before dawn, with nurses and patients aboard, the captain navigated through U.S. minefields to reach the Corregidor dock, just in time for an air raid on the island. As the nurses hopped off the boat, a truck arrived.

"They didn't even stop; they just grabbed us and hauled us on the truck and took us up to Malinta Tunnel," Madeline said. The fortified tunnel had been bored through the solid rock of Malinta Hill in the 1920s. It offered complete protection from artillery or air attack. The last bastion of defense in the Philippines, Corregidor was nicknamed "The Rock."

CHRISTMAS DAY

WHILE FELLOW NURSES EVACUATED FROM Sternberg, the hospital's commanding officer, Colonel J. W. Duckworth, called for Frances Nash. "Prepare yourself to be taken prisoner," he told her.

Frances might have laughed at the idea just weeks before. Now she knew the grim possibilities that faced her. "Yes, sir," she said. The colonel explained that she was to stay behind at Sternberg and continue her duties until all supplies and staff members had been evacuated.

Throughout the night and next day, Frances assisted in surgery, while the Japanese marched closer and closer to Manila.

Between operations Frances destroyed pa-perwork to keep it from enemy hands.

When the last remaining nurses and surgical staff at Sternberg received orders to flee, Frances crammed her pockets with narcotics, stimulants, and enough morphine pills to provide every Army nurse a lethal dose—a last resort if taken prisoner by an enemy known to have raped and tortured captives when invading China four years prior.

As long as the nurses felt their skills were useful, the tablets would remain secret. Some of the nurses would later hide the suicide pills inside rolls of their hair pinned at the back of their neck.

AT THE WATERFRONT FRANCES BOARDED A small steamer that zigzagged across Manila Bay. Flames from burning buildings onshore, ships ablaze in the harbor, and a brightly shining moon reflecting on the inky waters made the night almost as bright as day. Frances was so tired, she lay down on the deck, with her helmet and gas mask by her side.

At 1:00 A.M., as the steamer docked on Bataan, Japanese planes strafed and bombed the area. After disembarking, Frances spotted a chicken coop on the pier. Without thinking twice, she pushed the chickens out and squeezed in. When the raid eased a little, she and others from the boat scuttled into the jungle. For almost three hours she huddled in the first of many jungle foxholes, where tree rats scurried about, sometimes running shortcuts across her body.

Frances tested the chin strap on her helmet and brushed away bugs crawling over her. "You live a million years in each second in a foxhole," she said.

AT HOSPITAL NO. 1 NURSES WOKE AT SUNRISE Christmas Day and set to work. Poking through the warehouse for equipment, they discovered leftovers from the Great War. Iron hospital cots had grown rusty packed away in 1918 newspapers. Surgical instruments packed in petroleum jelly for safekeeping had to be cleaned with ether. After a day of scrubbing, scouring, and setting up, they had eighteen hospital wards of three dozen cots each.

The surgical staff divided themselves into teams including a surgeon, a second doctor, a nurse, and a medic. As they squared away the operating room, Frankie Lewey and Dr. Alfred Weinstein reacquainted themselves. Frankie had met the surgeon six months earlier, when they sailed for the Philippines on the same transport ship.

Sterilization of instruments and supplies became their first order of business. With no elec-

Army Nurse Frankie Lewey and Army surgeon Dr. Arthur Weinstein shipboard en route to the Philippines, 1941. They met again on Bataan at Hospital No. 1, where Frankie was a ward nurse.

tric sterilizer available, they used steel-jacketed pressure cookers heated by pressure-pumped Bunsen burners to clean huge piles of operating gowns, linen, gauze, towels, and swabs.

The long day ended with roast duck for Christmas dinner. Hattie Brantley kept an eye toward the entrance to Manila Bay. With a little luck, their primitive hospital wouldn't be needed. Surely help was on its way. Hattie expected a convoy of U.S. ships filled with sol-

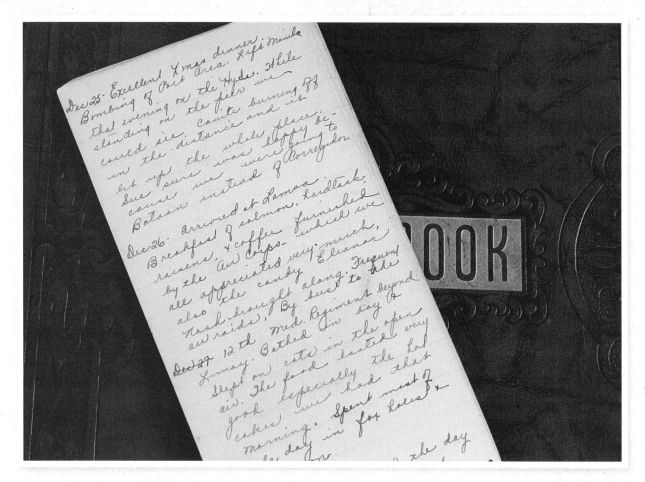

Dec 25- Excellent Xmas dinner. Bombing of Port Area. Left Manila that evening on the Hyde. While standing on the pier we could see, quite a distance off in the distance and it lit up the whole place. Sure sure was happy be- cause we were going to Bataan instead of Corregidor.

Dec 26- Arrived at Lamao Breakfast of salmon, hardtack, raisins, & coffee furnished by the air corps- which we all appreciated very much, also the candy Eleanor Nash brought along. Frequent air raids! By bus to the

Dec 27 12th med. Regiment beyond Limay. Bathed in day & slept on cots in the open air. The food tasted very good, especially the hot cakes we had that morning. Spent most of the day in fox holes & the day

diers, weapons, and supplies to rescue them "at least by tomorrow."

But the next day Japanese air raids on Mariveles Harbor at the tip of the Bataan Peninsula sent more than two hundred patients to Hospital No. 1. When Frances Nash arrived to oversee the operating room's eight tables, scores of wounded men waited their turn for surgery. "Anything the ambulances could pick up still living was brought to us," said Frances.

"Despite the confusion, Frances was supervising with an eagle eye," said Dr. Weinstein. "Our nurses drove themselves as if beset by devils until their neatly starched uniforms were crumpled, sweat-soaked rags. Frances especially was a dynamo, driving the med-

ics with her lashing tongue until they cussed her sullenly under their breaths—not openly, because they were sure they'd get the back of her hand."

Despite her colorful language, those Frances Nash supervised soon discovered she was a softie inside—kind, sympathetic, and understanding.

On December 28 President Roosevelt broadcast a speech to the Philippines. "I give to the people of the Philippines my solemn pledge that their freedom will be redeemed and their independence established and protected," he said. "The entire resources, in men and in material, of the United States stand behind that pledge."

Hattie Brantley did not hear the president's

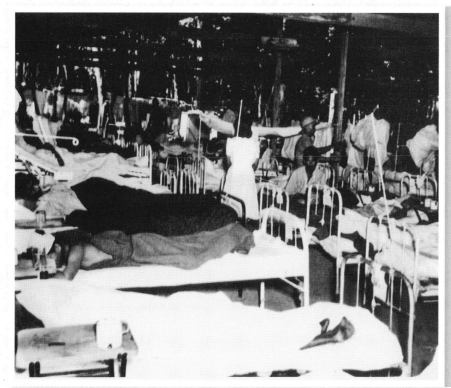

Opposite: Army Nurse Ethel Thor's diary entry for Christmas 1941, the evening she evacuated Manila for the Bataan Peninsula.

Left: Army nurses worked twenty-hour shifts caring for casualties on Bataan Peninsula, Philippine Islands.

Below: The wounded at a medical station in Bataan. Serious cases on litters were transported to Hospital No. 1, where they received a smear test for gangrene bacteria, treatment for shock, and surgery if needed. One of the men pictured is delirious, possibly from sunstroke.

speech on the radio. Hospital No. 1's eighteen wards overflowed with casualties from the front lines. "I'd get down on my knees, finally not even bothering to arise, but crawling to the next cot," Hattie said.

Every ward was a surgical ward. Hattie and the other ward nurses' main duty was to give morphine shots for pain relief. "The needles had to be sharpened on a piece of stone. Then you boiled the needle and you put a morphine tablet in the glass syringe and dumped in the water that you used to boil the needle to dissolve the morphine."

Hattie didn't have a moment to think of home or family. As a girl, she had been particularly close to her father, a truck farmer. She hadn't wanted her mother's life as a farm wife with half a dozen kids pulling at her skirt while she washed and cleaned and hoed the garden.

But she had wanted a horse. After earning her nursing degree, she figured that an army cavalry unit was her best bet to climb in the saddle. Hattie signed up, never dreaming she'd end up on a battlefield in a hospital where the nurses' station was a wooden crate turned on end.

At night, under blackout conditions due to air raids, the women carried flashlights covered with blue cellophane paper. The surgery, its lights shrouded from enemy eyes, ran around the clock.

The nurses worked twenty-hour shifts without complaining. "We evidenced faith, hope, and trust in God, in General MacArthur, in FDR, and in the U.S.A.," Hattie said. "In fact, anytime anyone looked in the direction of the bay and did not see a convoy steaming in, it was with disbelief!"

AS THE U.S. MILITARY FLED TO BATAAN, FOReign nationals, including some two thousand American civilians, remained stranded in Manila. The week after Christmas they stashed food and hid valuables. Reports indicated that Japanese troops headed to take over the city were making good time, some on bicycles! They were expected to arrive with the New Year.

New Year's Day came and went. A sign posted over Manila City Hall declared OPEN CITY. BE CALM.

This was proving difficult for Peggy Nash and ten other Navy nurses. Cañacao Hospital was so near prime Japanese targets—the navy yard, docks, and ships in the bay—that nurses had evacuated all their patients to Manila. Then they'd been sent to staff an annex hospital in a Manila college, Santa Scholastica.

Navy nurses realized that the U.S. forces had retreated and left them. They'd been stuck behind with the patients that were too ill to be moved. Anxiety turned to anger. Had they

been forgotten, or simply abandoned?

On January 2 Peggy heard a strange *putt-putt-putt-putt* in the streets. Japanese soldiers rode in on motorbikes and bicycles to take over the city. Looking out over the balcony and seeing the American Stars and Stripes coming down and the red sun of the Japanese flag going up was Peggy's worst moment yet.

The next day, Japanese officers came to talk with the U.S. Navy staff at Santa Scholastica. The Americans reminded them of the standards for humane treatment of POWs agreed to by world leaders at the 1929 Geneva Convention.

"We didn't sign it," their captors said.

Japanese soldiers surrounded the temporary hospital and nurses' quarters with barbed-wire barricades and posted sentries who made rounds day and night. Peggy concentrated on the needs of her patients. When the nurses realized that the Japanese planned to confiscate their drugs, they went to work mislabeling important antimalarial drugs as simple soda bicarbonate and thus saved them from the enemy.

One night two wounded Filipino soldiers on Peggy's ward made a break for home. But the Japanese had counted the patients. They realized the next morning that the men were missing. Peggy heard whispers about the guards threatening to shoot the corpsman and doctor on the ward if more patients escaped. The chief nurse didn't tell her for a week— Peggy had been on that list, too.

To her relief, no more prisoners disappeared. Though, as patients improved, the

Opposite: Japanese troops advance on Manila astride bicycles, which allowed quiet, flexible, inexpensive transport for thousands of soldiers. December 1941.

Above: All Filipino-American forces leave, and Manila is declared an "open city" in the hope of saving civilian lives and property from destruction. December 1941.

Japanese transferred them from the hospital to Manila's Bilibid Prison. Most still needed medical care, and Peggy believed many of them would die without it. It was frightening to be held captive by an enemy who seemed to value life so little.

CHAPTER 6
MAKE-DO MEDICINE

JANUARY 1941
U.S. Army General Hospital No. 2, South
Bank of the Real River, Bataan

Casualties swamped Hospital No. 1's surgical wards, so the Army sent bulldozers to clear space elsewhere in the jungle for a convalescent hospital. Army Nurse Josephine "Josie" Nesbit agreed to supervise the nursing staff at Hospital No. 2.

This was Josie's second tour of duty in the Philippines but her first in wartime. She served second to ANC Philippine Commander Maude Davison. Josie had a firm chin and a reputation for unyielding honesty. She seemed intimidating but was often more like a mother than a commander, which was why the Filipino nurses soon took to calling her "Mama Josie."

Josie followed ten miles of narrow trail from the coastal village of Mariveles to the site for the convalescent hospital. Enlisted men from the medical corps carried in blankets, sheets, pajamas, pillows, morphine, quinine, sulfa, and vitamins. They buried the drugs in deep trenches to protect them from enemy bombings.

Hospital No. 2 started out with five chairs and thirty tables. A local planter helped by hiring carpenters to construct more tables to hold supplies and for the mess, or meal service. Carpenters also made benches, beds, medicine cabinets, brooms, fly swatters, urinals, and laundry baskets, all from bamboo. Rice straw stuffed into mattress covers made surprisingly comfortable beds. The nurses arranged desks and medicine cabinets under stands of bamboo and acacia trees. One of a few pup tents kept medical records dry.

"We had a tent over the records, but no tent over the patients. I guess the Army thought the patients would dry out quicker than the records," Army Nurse Sally Blaine said.

Sally's first job was to set up the mess. The Army had retreated so fast, pans used for cooking at Sternberg had been carried over dirty. "We sat down in streams with these dirty pans, and we scoured them with rocks and sand," Sally said. That, however, was the least of her challenges.

"Women had a hard time going to the field with soldiers. . . . There was a sergeant who swore, 'I ain't going to have no damn woman tell me what to do in my kitchen.'"

Josie assigned Sally to set up wards, which quickly filled with patients. Bulldozers cleared underbrush to expand Hospital No. 2 along the Real River, which was a shallow stream in the current dry season. They left standing a canopy of mahogany, acacia, and bamboo for shade and to hide the sprawling hospital from Japanese planes. Soon Sally had set up seven wards among tangled vines and connected by jungle paths.

Opposite: Left to right: U.S. Army nurses Josie Nesbit, Maude Davison, and Helen Hennessey. Davison, the chief Army nurse in the Philippines and a World War I veteran, came over from headquarters on Corregidor Island to inspect the Bataan hospitals.

Top: Army Nurse Ethel "Sally" Blaine before the war.

Bottom: In the foreground, wounded Filipino soldiers eat at a jungle hospital on Bataan. American soldiers are shown at tables in the background.

"I cried at first every time we admitted patients," Sally said. "I would cry and cry when I heard one had died. Finally an older nurse said, 'Sally, you've got to stop this. You can't cry every time one dies, or you're going to be crying all the time.' So I got a grip on myself. I'm sure it affected a lot of us. But we didn't talk about it."

General MacArthur sent a message to Bataan from Corregidor on January 15:

> *Help is on the way from the United States.*
> *Thousands of troops and hundreds of planes are being dispatched. The exact time of arrival of reinforcements is unknown. . . .*
> *It is imperative that our troops hold until these reinforcements arrive.*
>
> *No further retreat is possible.*

Medical staff greeted the news with shouts, applause, hugging, and kissing. A bit later someone caught a radio newscast from San Francisco. President Roosevelt had promised that "the skies will be black with planes over your heads."

Still, the nurses' work continued under constant threat of falling enemy bombs. "We were the first nurses in the United States Army to be subjected to actual combat," said Josie. "On Bataan, there were simply no rear areas." Rear areas are typically safe places far enough behind the front line to avoid combat.

"The first time they told us to take cover, I did as I was told," said Sally. "When I looked up, I looked right into the eyes of a patient who couldn't move. I felt so ashamed that I got up. I never again threw myself down in the presence of my patients."

Josie Nesbit maintained morale by example. She knew hard work like an old friend. When she was born two days before Christmas 1894, hard times had a choke hold on the Nesbit farm near Butler, Missouri.

The seventh of ten children, Josie started her chores before daylight, and days stretched long, like a soybean row vanishing into the horizon. An orphan at age twelve, she lived with her grandmother and later a cousin, growing tall and big-boned, and needing size-thirteen shoes.

At sixteen, Josie left home for nurses' training. Four years after graduating, she enlisted as a reserve Army nurse. Peacetime military life offered many advantages. Josie would never go hungry again, and someone else cooked and did the dishes. The work was less grueling than farm labor and more interesting. As a young nurse Josie hiked the American Rockies, swam the Hawaiian surf, and rode a camel through Egypt's Valley of the Kings.

The younger women on Bataan appreciated Josie's compassion, and she did her best to replace personal items her "girls" had been forced to leave. Josie begged Air Corps pilots flying to outer Philippine islands to bring back shoes and underwear.

Josie also helped ensure some privacy for the women, procuring a number of army-issue canvas field shelters. She acquired sheets of burlap to section off a part of the jungle where

U.S. Army nurses at Hospital No. 2 bathe in a stream bordering the hospital.

the nurses slept. Upstream from the main camp, corpsmen built a burlap fence around a pile of rocks in the middle of the river so the nurses could bathe out of sight. They sat on the cool, wet rocks, water streaming over them.

It was one of the only places the women could relax. They washed off the blood and grime and stole a few moments away from pain and death.

Occasionally they might sing a popular song. "You are my sunshine, my only sunshine . . ." or play together, splashing in the water. A large tree root growing from the stream bank formed a natural water slide, a place to ease tension, to shout and laugh, even as gunfire sounded through the jungle.

One afternoon Nurse Maude "Denny" Williams had the pool to herself. Hearing a rustle in the bushes, she feared a peeping Tom. But it was flying steel peppering the leaves of a ban-

yan tree. An enemy plane swooped low, its gunner firing away. Denny leapt from the water. Hiding under a bush, she prayed for her life.

A ten-year veteran Army nurse anesthetist, Denny had resigned two years earlier to marry William "Bill" Williams, a Caltex Oil Company executive in Manila. When the war started, Maude Davison had immediately asked Denny back to work at Sternberg Hospital. Bill joined the Army as it retreated to Bataan, and Denny joined the nurses working at Hospital No. 2.

When the bullets stopped flying, she grabbed her clothes and went back to work.

"Did you hear about Denny being strafed?" The story spread. "She didn't want to die with only her dog tags on." Denny laughed with her friends, but that moment under the bush, she'd faced the facts. Some nurses still believed they'd be rescued. "Common sense told me we were involved in a dire disaster here."

DAYS STRETCHED INTO WEEKS. EVERYONE WENT
on half rations. Heavy fighting continued. In
one thirty-six-hour stretch the surgical teams
at Hospital No. 1 performed 420 operations.

At Hospital No. 2, one nurse had a small
radio. At night the nurses gathered to listen to
the Voice of Freedom, a U.S. military broadcast
from Corregidor, or KGEI San Francisco. Near
the end of January they heard about the first
American convoy to head overseas since Pearl
Harbor. Ships carrying troops and ammunition
had just landed—in Northern Ireland. Where

were MacArthur's promised reinforcements to
the Philippines?

The fighting raged closer. When the front
line came within fifteen miles of Hospital
No. 1, the order came to move back. Nurses
packed supplies and equipment and loaded
patients into trucks.

The new site for Hospital No. 1, a former
motor pool and repair shop, was on the East
Road near the tip of the peninsula. The place
was cool and breezy and shaded by leafy hard-
wood trees. Frances Nash and her crew turned
the one wood-frame building in the center of
the compound into an operating pavilion.

At Hospital No. 2, when the patient load
reached two thousand, twenty-eight nurses
transferred in from Fort Mills Hospital on
Corregidor to help. Even patients lent a hand.
Two men, each missing one arm, learned to
work together rolling bandages.

Still, nurses worked twenty hours a day.
They began each morning carrying water
from Real River to bathe their patients. They
cleaned wounds, applied sulfa powder, changed
dressings, and gave morphine shots.

"There's not much we could do for them,"
Millie Dalton said later. "There's no way of
actually keeping things clean much in the
jungle."

Millie's ticket to nursing school had been a
winning essay she wrote for a newspaper con-
test as a teenager. A woman journalist from
the paper later offered to lend Millie money for
training at Grady Memorial Hospital in Atlanta.
But nothing she experienced at Grady prepared
Millie for the helplessness she felt now.

Opposite: A letter that Army Nurse Dorothy Scholl wrote to her family from Bataan. In early February mail was still getting out of Bataan, with Air Corps pilots making supply runs to the outer Philippine Islands.

Above: Hospital No. 1, on Bataan, is marked as a medical and noncombatant facility by the red cross on the tin roof and another cross on the tarpaulin spread on the ground in front of the hospital, partially shown at right.

"Seeing these soldiers with no place to go, and not able to get out of the way of anything," Millie said. "It was devastating to watch."

Sally Blaine spent four hours taking the temperatures of two hundred men in an orthopedic ward.

"I finally said to my ward officer, 'What's the sense of taking temperatures? No one will ever read the records.' If you saw a man had a high fever and chill[s], you didn't need a thermometer to tell you he needed quinine."

Her ward officer agreed, and they stopped taking temperatures.

Hospital No. 2 was no longer limited to convalescents. Surgical patients came straight from brutal hand-to-hand fighting on the front line to No. 2's operating room—a bamboo pavilion open to weather and any bug or bit of nature that flew in.

Ethel Thor supervised the operating theater with a subtle sense of humor and serene manner, keeping patients moving in and out as quickly as possible. Nurses assisted at three surgery tables and two debridement tables. Surgeons debrided, or sliced away, dead tissue from burns and shrapnel wounds, or even live tissue when that was the only way to halt blood loss. Ethel remained unruffled, except when a patient screamed in pain because hurried doctors sliced before the anesthesia took effect.

The dwindling drug supply worried Ethel. Nurses resorted to ether for sedation, "going back to Civil War times."

On breaks, Ethel sometimes took advantage of the lights in the surgery to sit and read. She kept a small journal, noting events in sparse words. She wrote home to her sister and nieces on February 5:

> *Hello folks,*
> *Just a line to let you know everything's OK. Two meals a day but we usually manage to get a few snacks between meals. The two things I miss are good coffee and rolls (that's in the line of food). Just like a camping trip—dirt, bugs and everything else that goes with it. Do my own washing and still manage to get a bath every day. . . . Don't worry as our Uncle Sam is taking care of us.*

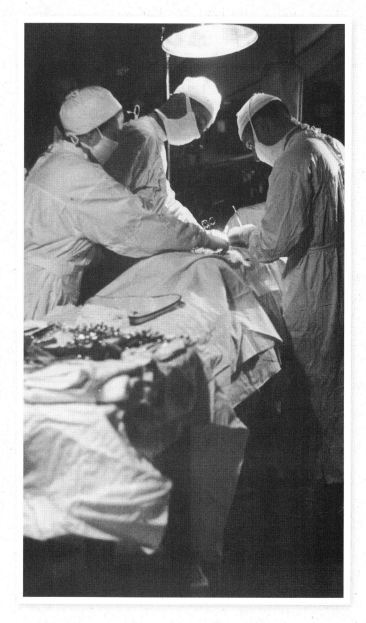

While primitive conditions and lack of medicine challenged the nurses' professional standards, enemy patients tested their ethics. The women loathed the Japanese soldiers and disliked treating prisoner-of-war patients. But they gave all the wounded their best care and treated them with compassion.

One such prisoner had a badly set broken arm, which doctors decided to rebreak and reset. As the anesthetist tried to put the Japanese man to sleep, he jumped off the table shrieking, "Don't kill me. Please don't kill me!" The interpreter translated.

Corpsmen grabbed the Japanese soldier and held him down, while nurses tried to make him understand he was safe. He struggled and cried until the anesthetic took effect. When he woke after the procedure, no interpreter was needed. "He seized our hands and hissed and jabbered his gratitude and amazement; it

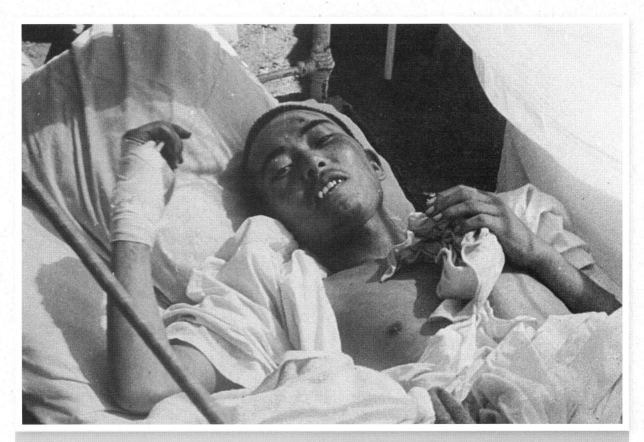

Opposite: An operating room under a tent at Hospital No. 2. Doctors try to save a near hopeless case shot in the neck, apparently severing the spinal cord. Lieutenant Colonel Jack Schwartz (left) operates, with Captain Paul S. Roland and Army Nurse Ethel Thor assisting. During the operation, a bomb landed nearby. Doctors paused until the ground and table stopped shaking, then continued.

Above: A twenty-two-year-old Japanese patient who expected to be shot gets fine treatment instead. Enemy soldiers received the same medical attention from nurses and doctors as the American soldiers did.

was pitiful, and somehow embarrassing," said Army Nurse Juanita Redmond.

The battle on Bataan raged into February. ANC Commander Maude Davison transferred five more nurses from Corregidor to help Josie Nesbit at Hospital No. 2. One of them, Ruth Straub, kept a diary.

February 11
More dogfighting overhead. Our main dan-ger—Oh, just as I am writing, the [Japanese] dropped bombs nearby. Much

more of this and we'll all be nervous wrecks. To continue, our main danger is shrapnel from our own antiaircraft. Yesterday, a piece went through a mattress. Fortunately, the patient had just left his bed. . . . Here they come again. Whew! Where is all the bravery I thought I possessed?

February 12
A huge iguana kept prowling through the underbrush by my bed. Sounded like it might be a sniper.

February 16
Eight of us jumped into a small foxhole in a raid today and nearly killed each other. One of the cooks was shot through the head. . . . Rats are chewing up our clothes.

Ten days later, a rat crawled into bed with Army Nurse Rita Palmer and bit her. Luckily, the wound wasn't serious.

"Mostly, you were scared to death you were going to get bit by a snake," Millie Dalton said. "I went to bed one night and had to get a gecko out of my bed."

There seemed no end to the horrors and indignities of an open-air jungle hospital. Poor sanitation became a health hazard. Thousands of people relied on rudimentary latrines. Dysentery "accidents" on the way to the latrines were common.

"In the jungle heat the stench was terrible," said one nurse. "When the toilet paper was almost gone, we could only give everyone two small sections with a tiny piece of soap. Most relied on nature's leaves. It was so ridiculous that at times we would laugh."

Maggots appeared along the paths on the ground. Flies and mosquitoes carried the dysentery everywhere. While nurses ate, they used one hand to wave flies away from their food. A soldier managed a joke about it. "FDR said the sky would be black with them. Did he mean flies instead of planes?"

CHAPTER 7
BOXED IN ON BATAAN

FEBRUARY–MARCH 1942
Bataan Peninsula

I n mid-February an eerie silence fell in Bataan. Japanese bombers and fighters stopped flying overhead. Invading troops fell back. With no new casualties, nurses took a breath. The reprieve from constant danger allowed them to have a little fun. One group went to the beach for a picnic and swimming.

Another day nurses attended a masquerade ball in the officers' mess. They shared whatever clothing they had carried from Manila and wore makeup and perfume. Someone scavenged an old, hand-wound, portable phonograph and a pile of records to play music for dancing.

The American men enjoyed the break, too. Lieutenant John P. Burns, 21st Pursuit Squadron, wrote in his diary:

March 3, 1942
As a morale booster, General George [M. Parker] had arranged the party, to which he invited nurses from Bataan Hospital No. 2. . . . Cpl. Greenman pounded out boogie-woogie on the old piano as they

danced with the 12 nurses who had accepted the invitation.

Unbeknownst to the nurses, Japan's Lieutenant General Masaharu Homma knew U.S. forces were growing short of food and ammunition and were too weak to attack. He pulled his men back to rest, recuperate, and prepare—to finish off the Americans.

The lull in fighting allowed U.S. soldiers to hike from their camps and visit nurses they were sweet on. Some proposed marriage. Several nurses said yes, including Rita Palmer, who had fallen in love with Navy Lieutenant Edwin Nelson of Huntington, West Virginia. He gave her a jade ring he'd bought in China for his mother. Army regulations required nurses who married to leave the service. If only!

Rita had happily left behind the decorous New England restraint of Hampton, New Hampshire, where she had grown up. Now she longed for home. Awakening on the morning of March 12, Rita heard that General MacArthur and his staff had left Corregidor for safety in Australia. MacArthur told reporters:

> *The President of the United States ordered me . . . to proceed to Australia for the purpose, as I understand it, of organizing the American offensive against Japan. . . . I shall return.*

Some nurses and soldiers on Bataan believed that their commander had deserted them. Others argued that the United States couldn't risk the Japanese capturing General MacArthur.

In either case, humor was the balm. "I am going to the latrine," Bataan soldiers cracked when nature called, "but I shall return."

Others sang lyrics composed to the tune of "The Battle Hymn of the Republic."

> *Dugout Doug's not timid, he's just cautious, not afraid.*
> *He's protecting carefully the stars that Franklin made.*
> *Four-star generals are rare as good food on Bataan,*
> *And his troops go starving on.*

When General Jonathan Wainwright replaced MacArthur, he estimated that only 25 percent of his Bataan soldiers were combat-effective. Wainwright himself walked with a cane, his legs hurting and weak from beriberi, a disease caused by lack of thiamine, or vitamin B1.

Sharp skirmishes along the Bataan front ended the temporary peace on March 22. Sixty Japanese bombers barraged Bataan day and night. Long-range heavy artillery fired from Cavite, strengthening the air attacks plastering Corregidor.

Wainwright ordered normal radio communications from Corregidor temporarily curtailed so that U.S. soldiers could transmit thirty thousand applications for government life insurance policies.

Disease struck as many soldiers as Japanese bombs, bullets, and bayonets did. From March to April, malaria cases increased from five hundred a day to nearly one thousand. Quinine, the only drug available to treat the disease in 1942, became too scarce to do much good.

Woozy and weak with malaria, Sally Blaine managed her ward from a cot. When Army Nurse Lucy Wilson became too sick to stand, she braced herself upright to assist in surgery by squeezing her arm into a gap by the operating table. A surgeon, scalpel in hand, convulsed with malarial chills.

Besides malaria, soldiers, doctors, and nurses alike suffered dysentery, dengue fever, and beriberi, all aggravated by the growing problem of malnutrition. As illness and battle wounds increased, food grew scarce. Canned fruit, vegetables, milk, rice, beans, flour, coffee, and cocoa gave way to whatever could be bought from local farmers or hunted.

As the Japanese forced Filipino-American troops to retreat farther into the jungle, the

soldiers drove the native carabao ahead of them. The carabao meat was tough and had a strong taste. Camp cooks tried different recipes to help the meat go down easier. One recipe suggested, "You put a rock in the cooking pot with the meat and when the rock melts, the carabao is tender."

Ethel Thor wrote home with the attitude characteristic of most of the nurses:

Hello,
Getting along OK. . . . Now and then we have carabao to eat, which really doesn't taste very bad—in fact, we can't tell whether it's beef or carabao.

A bulldozer cleared another large patch to expand Hospital No. 2 once again. Nurses put the wounded to bed on pieces of canvas and thatched mats on the ground. Sally Blaine paused to notice the thousands of sick and bleeding men spread on the ground in every direction.

Bataan writhed through its third month of

battle. The chief nurse at Hospital No. 1 told nurses, "We've got to make what we have last. If necessary we'll have one meal every two days. I know you won't complain."

Monkeys and lizards disappeared into stew pots, and the quartermaster, in charge of distributing food to the troops and medical units, butchered the last of 250 cavalry horses and forty-eight pack mules. A fighting man's food shrank from January's half ration to one-quarter, below one thousand calories a day, mostly gummy rice supplemented by anything they could find in the jungle, even python eggs.

Ruth Straub confided to her diary,

Lately I have been having nightmares. I am always stealing heads of fresh lettuce from dead men.

But nurses preferred the gnawing in their stomachs to the bite of the questions asked by the young men in their care.

"What'll happen to us if help doesn't come?"

"Am I going to make it?"

"Most of us followed a middle course, ducking the question or avoiding a direct answer," Dr. Weinstein said. "If a patient looked like he might kick the bucket, we called in the chaplain to give him last rites, collect personal mementos, and write last messages. . . . More often than not, soldiers didn't have to be told."

Nurses pushed themselves beyond imagination as April arrived. Hospital No. 2 distended two and a half miles. Nineteen wards spread along the Real River, connected by foot trails snaking under the shade of banyan trees, over rocks and roots, and through groves of bamboo. The air hung heavy with yellow acacia pollen, gunpowder sulfur, and the moans, cries, and silence of more than four thousand sick and suffering men.

Josie Nesbit accepted the inevitable, though she did not voice it. The Americans were losing.

"The battle was so close we could hear the detonations and feel concussions from the big artillery," said Denny Williams. "Bombs dropped every few minutes, and we grew used to the whistle of flying steel. Used to it, but never indifferent, only so tired and starved, we walked like zombies. Most of us expected to be taken prisoner right where we were. And yet . . . nobody really gave up."

Filipino-American soldiers were fast running out of ammunition, but Lieutenant General Homma's army grew stronger. For every Japanese soldier the Allies killed, hundreds came fresh from Japan to replace them, along with new artillery and squadrons of aerial bombers.

For Christians, April 3 was Good Friday. For the Japanese it was the anniversary of the death of their legendary first emperor, Jimmu. They honored his spirit by launching a massive artillery assault, with 150 pieces of artillery—guns, howitzers, mortars—pounding American and Filipino positions. Three thousand casualties deluged Hospital No. 2 that day.

The Monday morning after Easter, Rita Palmer was tending patients in her ward when the Japanese bombed Hospital No. 1. Ten bombs fell, one hitting the red cross in the center yard that declared the hospital and people inside were unarmed. One exploded directly on a ward. Another landed at the entrance to the hospital, blowing up a passing ammunition truck, which in turn decimated a bus full of wounded just then arriving.

"I remember coming to and having long beams of the roof over me and struggling out from under those," Rita said. "I have no idea how long I was knocked out. . . . I didn't even know about the piece of shrapnel in my chest for several hours. It didn't penetrate my lung. I had shrapnel in my legs, too."

The concussion hurled Juanita Redmond to the ground. She gasped for air. Her eyes felt as if they were being gouged from their sockets. Her body felt swollen and torn apart by violent pressure.

"This is the end, I thought," Juanita said. "There were mangled bodies under the ruins; a bloodstained hand stuck up through a pile of scrap; arms and legs had been ripped off and flung among the rubbish. Some of the mangled torsos were impossible to identify."

Dust, smoke, and screams filled the air. Nurses dove in, tearing through the debris in search of live patients. A corpsman climbed a tree to bring down a body blown into the top branches next to blankets and pajamas.

Hattie Brantley ran into the orthopedic ward for help and found a chaplain standing on a desk reciting the Lord's Prayer. Blood streamed down his arms and chest from a shrapnel wound.

Frances Nash, unscathed, shook with anger. "One of the wards hit contained thirty or more head cases, boys without eyes, ears, or noses. I had never before been so mad at any individual that I wanted to kill him, as I did the Japanese. I was so mad that I wasn't frightened."

The Japanese claimed that bombing the hospital was an accident. Some nurses didn't believe it.

Only sixty-five beds remained intact at Hospital No. 1. Seventy-three men had been killed, 117 further wounded by the bombs. No nurses died. Rita and another nurse injured in the attack were evacuated to Corregidor that night.

The bodies of the dead were stored until nightfall. Then a chaplain went with the grave-digging detail into the jungle. Due to the increasing number of corpses, a bulldozer dug a common grave. Frances had seen soldiers die, but nothing hit her like the night she visited a newly dug burial site to collect dog tags. "I never went back again. Too much for me, got to thinking I may be next."

NURSES AT BOTH HOSPITALS STARTED TO SEE symptoms of protein deficiency in soldiers' wasting muscles and protruding bones. Only enough food remained for each soldier to eat a few mouthfuls. Then the food was gone. With no fresh water available on the front lines, thirsty soldiers drank whatever water they could find, then showed up at the hospital sick from bacteria and dehydrated from dysentery.

The wounded appeared barefoot, their uniforms in rags. Wide-eyed with dread, they told of the enemy charging them shouting, "Banzai! Banzai!"—Japanese for "Long live the Emperor." Soldiers staggered into the hospital, laid down their rifles, and begged for food.

The last line of Filipino-American defense fragmented on April 8, three miles north of Hospital No. 2. The Japanese coiled for a final strike. The emaciated, outnumbered Filipino-American force would be pushovers. The Japanese knew it. The War Department in Washington, D.C., knew it. General MacArthur knew it. Still, he radioed from his headquarters in Australia, "There must be no thought of surrender."

Army Nurse Anna Williams (no relation to Denny Williams) climbed the hill behind Hospital No. 2. "I wanted to see what was happening, because the guns were closer and closer, and the smoke was thick," she said. "I'll never forget the dejection and the sadness and the awful look on the men as they came along the road, retreating, covered in bandages and blood and dirt."

"Quit worrying!" Josie Nesbit told herself. "Just accept what comes."

Opposite: An American patient gets open-incision treatment. After running out of antitoxin for gas gangrene, doctors improvised. Allowing sunlight and oxygen to penetrate the wound destroyed the anaerobic bacteria consuming the flesh.

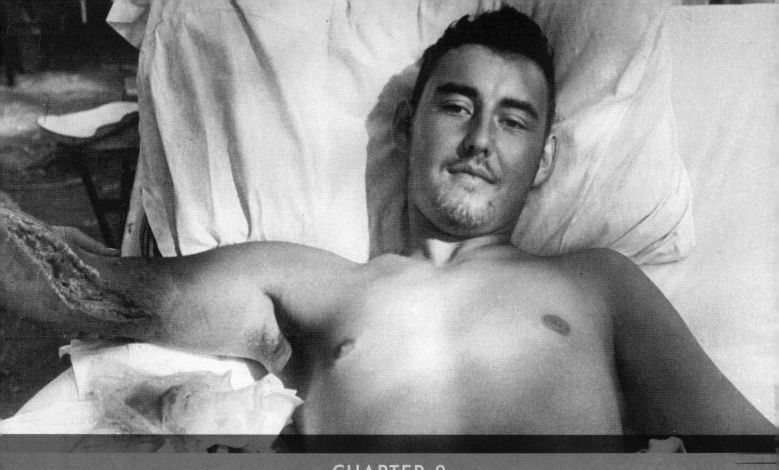

CHAPTER 8
RETREAT TO THE ROCK

The day came straight from hell—hot, never-ending, drenched with the smell of blood, and accompanied by erratic drumbeats of artillery fire and a discordant orchestra of rifle shots, groans, and cries of agony. When night fell at Hospital No. 2, Denny Williams had been on her feet in surgery for forty-eight hours with little to eat. She heard a medical officer swear. "Hell, it'll have to be a surrender, or the worst massacre in his-

tory. . . . We haven't anything left to fight with except coconuts and bamboo sticks."

Colonel James O. Gillespie summoned Josie Nesbit and told her that General Wainwright had ordered the nurses to evacuate to Corregidor. "Tell your American nurses to get down here to my office by twenty hundred hours," he said, "and only bring whatever they can carry in their hands."

"What about my Filipino nurses?" Josie asked.

"Only the *American* nurses."

Josie could not help remembering the

Filipina nurse Gregoria Espinosa worked with the American nurses and became friends with Frankie Lewey.

reports of Chinese women raped and killed when the Imperial Army conquered the city of Nanking, and she worried about the Filipinas who called her Mama Josie.

"If my Filipino nurses don't go," she said, "I'm. Not. Going."

Josie waited long minutes while Colonel Gillespie called Wainwright's headquarters. "All right," the Colonel finally told her. "All the nurses will go."

Several minutes later, Ethel Thor and Denny Williams were among the nurses assisting doctors in the operating "room" when Josie walked in. "Take off your gloves and gowns," she told them. "You're leaving." Ethel didn't move.

"*Now!*" Josie said.

Hundreds of wounded men lay waiting for surgery. Ethel believed she had been put on earth for one reason: to serve others in need. Abandoning patients to the enemy devastated her. Most of the women were appalled at the order to leave, and refused to go. Josie made it clear they had no choice.

Many stayed with their patients until the last minute before going to pack. In her anguish over leaving, one nurse forgot the bracelet that served as her engagement ring. Another abandoned her underwear on a clothesline. One nurse threw wet laundry into a pillowcase to go, while another came along with curlers in her hair. A nurse left behind her beloved Bible and her copy of Emerson's poetry. Others left letters, photographs, and souvenirs of happier times in Manila.

Denny's husband, Bill Williams, had just been admitted to Hospital No. 2 that morning. She ran down the path to the officers' ward, where he lay sick with malaria.

"We're leaving," she whispered. "It's supposed to be a secret from the patients. Bill, I don't want to go."

"Of course you're going," he whispered.

"No. Do I have to go?"

"Yes, you have to go." Neither of them could voice all the things they wanted to say. Denny kissed him and ran back through the darkness, arriving just in time to answer Josie's roll call.

Frankie Lewey didn't say good-bye to anyone. She hung her head, hiding tears as she carried her bag along the edge of the hospital, where the wounded lay among the trees. She kept her back to the patients she called her "boys." That way, she told herself, "they won't see me go."

"Nurse . . . ?" one called out.

Frankie paused.

"Nurse?"

She couldn't ignore the soldier. She'd do what she could for him in these last moments. He wanted to talk. Told her his name, his hometown.

"Please take this," he said, holding out a ring that had been his mother's. He didn't want the Japanese to get it.

"Take it," he said. "Remember me."

The ring felt heavy in Frankie's hand. A weight she would carry forever.

AT HOSPITAL NO. 1 FRANCES NASH, HATTIE Brantley, and the other dozen nurses boarded a bus and trundled along the crowded coast road. American troops headed in the opposite direction, toward the enemy. Thousands of them trudged along in weary columns. Starving soldiers begged for food as the bus inched along. The sight was excruciating for the nurses, as they had nothing to give them and knew that the men would be Japanese prisoners the next day. Finally, the bus reached the Mariveles Harbor docks. The nurses squeezed into a launch and sailed for Corregidor.

THE EIGHTY-EIGHT NURSES FROM HOSPITAL No. 2 had more trouble reaching the docks, where they were scheduled to catch a boat at 2:00 A.M. The Army motor pool scrounged ambulances, staff cars, a bus, and trucks for the evacuation, but in the confusion some nurses were left to find their own transportation. Several ended up riding in a garbage truck and getting stuck in bomb craters along the way. Passing soldiers pushed them out. Filipino villagers, carrying their earthly goods and running from the Japanese, clogged the roads. Some pounded on the nurses' bus, begging for a ride.

Two nurses had to hitch a ride when the car they were in broke down. Other nurses had to wait when their vehicles ran out of gas. One car stopped to let American troops march by. Midnight passed. Nurses heard soldiers calling out to one another in the night and small-arms fire in the jungle. The Japanese advanced close by, and nurses could hear them hollering "Banzai!" as shells arched overhead. Dynamite explosions filled the sky with thunder and flashes of fire, as U.S. troops demolished weapons, vehicles, and ammunition dumps to keep them from enemy hands.

BOOM!

The largest blast yet shook the earth. Nurses covered their aching ears. It seemed the whole world was going up in flames. One of the largest stocks of ammunition had blown just as a truck carrying a group of nurses approached.

Everything on wheels ground to a stop. Army Nurse Minnie Breese was sick with malaria and dysentery. Shaking with chills and fever, she climbed from the truck bed and lay next to the road without the strength to

On the morning of April 9, American officers pass through enemy lines along Bataan's East Road. Their job is to locate a Japanese officer and deliver a message: The Americans wanted to surrender.

care whether she lived or died. It was at least an hour before the fire burned low and traffic moved again. Minnie's friends helped her back into the truck.

By now the convoy of nurses from Hospital No. 2 had fragmented into individual vehicles struggling to get to Mariveles. As a result, nurses arrived by different routes and at different times, and found their own transport across the water to Corregidor. A group including Ethel Thor arrived at about 5:30 that morning. The evacuation boat had left while it was still dark, to protect the nurses already on board from air attack. With dawn now breaking over the wharf, Japanese planes indeed began to bomb the area, making it more difficult for boats to dock, load, or depart. Ethel's group sought cover in a Navy tunnel, where they found canned peaches, tomato juice, and corned beef left behind by U.S. forces.

When Sally Blaine's group arrived, they saw no other nurses, but spotted a U.S. officer on the dock.

"Hey, you!" Sally yelled, running across the sand toward him. "Where's the boat that the nurses are supposed to go over on?"

"It came and left."

"What are we going to do?"

"How many are you?" he asked.

"Five."

"I can take you." The officer loaded the nurses into a small craft with an outboard motor.

As they sailed, the water appeared silvery gold in the calm of early morning. Sally looked at the sky and the water and thought it might be the last sunrise she'd see.

"We didn't talk. During all that time we didn't cry, scream, or carry on. You were quiet. You kept your fears to yourself."

Seventy thousand American and Philippine men surrender unconditionally to the Japanese Imperial Army. It is the largest U.S. Army surrender in history. Bataan Peninsula, April 9, 1942.

JOSIE NESBIT DID NOT ARRIVE UNTIL AFTER 6:00 A.M., when Filipino-American forces on Bataan surrendered to the Japanese. She discovered Ethel's group waiting for a boat and went in search of a telephone to call headquarters on Corregidor and request help. Collapsing with exhaustion, a number of the nurses slept. Others waited fitfully. Had they been abandoned?

Several hours passed before a boat came to take them across the bay. Japanese dive bombers attacked, shattering the dock just as the boat pulled away. Ethel and the others crouched low, huddling under canvas.

Except for Anna Williams. As they sped across the water, zigzagging to avoid falling bombs, Anna filed her nails. "There wasn't anything else to do, and I wasn't going to sit and moan."

When they reached Corregidor, several nurses were too weak to get up the hill to the safety of Malinta Tunnel on their own. No worries, though; they leaned on their comrades.

"My God, look at them," said a soldier.

"The fact we all got there and no nurse was lost is just a miracle," Hattie Brantley said.

The first nurses to arrive on Corregidor from Bataan had piled two to a bunk, able to give in to their weariness for the first time in over three months.

By the time Millie Dalton made it to Corregidor, there were no beds. "So I lay down on the concrete floor with my helmet for a pillow, and I went to sleep. I was that exhausted."

CHAPTER 9

HOLING UP ON CORREGIDOR ISLAND

APRIL 1942
Malinta Tunnel, Corregidor Island

The Japanese could bomb day and night, but they could not blast through the three hundred feet of rock and soil above Malinta Tunnel. The eighty-six Army nurses, twenty-six Filipino nurses, and one Navy nurse on Corregidor were safe. And there was food—more and better than the women had eaten in six weeks.

Though the hospital was situated underground, its equipment and staff's expertise rivaled any in the world. The hospital lay in a tunnel branch the length of a football field. One end opened to the outside, wide enough for two ambulances to drive in, where nurses met them for triage. Stretcher-bearers carried the wounded to the surgical wards located in eight smaller offshoots of the main hospital. Aboveground generators provided electricity, a cold-storage depot preserved food, and a chlorination plant ensured safe drinking water.

The subterranean network of corridors was like a small city, with areas for eating and sleeping, kitchen and laundry, a barber and general store. Off-duty Army officers in shirt-sleeves, Navy officers in shorts, enlisted men in jeans, and convalescents in white pajamas gathered at the canteen to listen to news on the radio, play cards, and exchange rumors.

The women settled in under the blue mercury-vapor lights, but they continued to worry about the men they had left on Bataan. They had no word from them. Neither did the American public, who would not find out what happened to the men who surrendered on Bataan for nearly two years.

The Japanese marched those American and Filipino POWs sixty-five miles north to Camp O'Donnell in the hot sun, with little food or water. No one knows for sure how many men died in the six days that came to be called the Bataan Death March—perhaps as many as twenty thousand. Another roughly forty thousand POWs are believed to have died in the sixty days after the men reached Camp O'Donnell.

The 8,800 patients at Hospitals No. 1 and No. 2 did not march to Camp O'Donnell. Two thousand Filipino patients were released by the Japanese to go home, but many were seriously wounded. Hundreds of their bodies were seen by villagers along the East Road, where they died or were killed. American patients remained in the Bataan hospitals for two months before being trucked to prison camps. Two out of every three American soldiers alive at the time of the Bataan surrender did not live to go home.

When the nurses came to Corregidor, twelve thousand people crowded the small

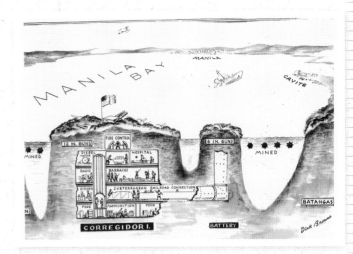

Opposite: The west entrance to Malinta Tunnel on Corregidor Island, with San Jose Barrio in the foreground. Tramway tracks run from the dock through the tunnel to carry personnel and supplies, c. 1937.

Top: A period drawing of Malinta Tunnel on Corregidor Island.

Bottom: American soldiers being directed by a Japanese soldier. On the march to Camp O'Donnell, the Japanese shot, bayoneted, or beheaded men who fell behind or broke ranks to grab food or slurp water from buffalo wallows. Under surrender terms, the Japanese agreed to treat prisoners humanely, but they underestimated the number of POWs they would need to feed and transport.

island—seven thousand combat troops, two thousand civilians, and three thousand military administrators and medical personnel. Air raids drove everyone except the fighting men underground. People slept along each side of the tunnel on ammunition cases, cots, or the cement floor, where ambulances passed within inches of their heads. Civilians crowded into the subterranean barracks. Nurses' quarters were in a tunnel next to the hospital.

Madeline Ullom began to feel like one of the rats that scurried about in the hot, stuffy tunnels. Burrowed under Corregidor, nurses lost track of day and night.

Red lights flashed, warning of air raids. Bombs fell, shaking the rock walls and ceiling, from the main entrance to the farthest lateral branch. Each blast released particles of concrete and clouds of dust, which the ventilation system, when it was working, only seemed to recycle. The stench of sweat, blood, disinfectants, anesthetics, overused latrines, and wounds with decomposing flesh could gag a person.

"It was like being in a steel bucket with somebody beating on the outside with a hammer," said Hattie Brantley. When the electricity went out, corpsmen held flashlights for the surgical teams. "The darkness was . . . so thick, you could feel it."

Walls and ceiling shook, medicine bottles toppled, bunk beds scooted. Most of the nurses remained calm and proficient under Maude Davison's and Josie Nesbit's supervision. April marched on in a suffocating haze. Food and medical supplies dwindled.

After they captured Bataan, the Japanese intensified their attack on the American battalions dug in on Corregidor's beaches. Each raid sent hundreds of wounded to the hospital. Nurses remained professional, even when seeing friends and acquaintances coming in on the stretchers.

In the cramped hospital tunnels of Corregidor, neither the living nor the dying had privacy. The patient load increased; double-stacked beds became triples. Nurses climbed on the foot rails to care for men on the top tier and change the bedding. Then a bomb hit the laundry facility, and there were no more clean sheets. Fifteen hundred patients soon filled tunnels meant for five hundred.

Exhausted nurses battled their own illnesses: dysentery they contracted on Bataan and dengue fever. Sally Blaine suffered continuing bouts of malaria. Perspiration coupled with filth and malnutrition caused the women to break out in large puffy water blisters, which smarted, itched, and could turn into sores and become infected. Nurses who spent hours lifting and reaching likened the pain and misery to a plague.

When they had the chance, nurses slipped outside Malinta's entrance to snatch a few minutes of fresh air. A quick glance at the sunrise, precious moments under the stars, or the feel of a breeze and sun on one's cheeks helped them bear up. Frankie Lewey admitted to gazing over the water to the horizon, hoping to see the tall masts of ships arriving to rescue them.

Aerial attacks stopped in the evenings, and the chance of securing a little elbow room and a deep breath was hard to resist. As darkness fell on April 25, dozens of men gathered outside near the tunnel's west entrance. When a shell hit close by, they ran for the tunnel. But the concussion slammed the iron entrance gate closed and jammed it. As the men pounded on the bars, yelling for help, another shell whistled down, exploding right at the tunnel entrance.

Nurses heard the men's shrieks and sprinted to help. Through the smoke and dust they

glimpsed chunks of flesh and bone scattered in the tunnel. The blast had propelled body parts through the slats of the jammed gate.

Corpsmen pried open the gate, and nurses, fighting shock and nausea, started triage. "Deaths from shock mounted no matter how frantically we worked over the victims," Juanita Redmond said. "The litter-bearers kept bringing in more and more. Once, as I stooped to give an injection to one . . . I saw that it was a headless body. Shock and horror made me turn furiously on the corpsmen.

"'Must you do this?' I cried.

"'It's so dark out there,' one of the men stammered. 'We can't use lights. We feel for the bodies and just roll them onto the stretchers.'"

Another soldier carried in had his leg hanging by shreds of skin from his thigh. Through gritted teeth, he told Juanita, "Don't cut off . . . my clothes . . . got no underpants on."

The attack killed fourteen men instantly. Nurses and doctors worked all night trying to save the rest, more than one hundred seriously wounded. Busy doctors turned minor surgeries over to nurses.

Though confronted by carnage from the first day of the war, the nurses never became hardened to shattered and bleeding bodies. That night they tightened tourniquets and treated shock with tears streaming down their faces. Most had learned to draw upon a "blessed numbness" that allowed them to do their job. But when faced with such mass suffering and death, something cracks inside the human soul. Juanita said, "You can't ever be quite the same again."

Josie Nesbit believed that her charges kept going, in part, because there was no place to hide and no way to escape.

Four days later Nurse Dorothy Scholl shared her birthday, April 29, with Japan's Emperor Hirohito. She had no party, but Japanese forces celebrated with the heaviest bombardment yet to hit Corregidor. Bombers from the air and artillery from Bataan and Cavite pounded the island for twelve hours straight. The Japanese planes flew too high for the Americans to shoot down.

Nurse Alice "Swish" Zwicker wrote in her diary:

It's a strange thing about war. One never gets used to it and yet once it begins it seems always to have been that way. No beginning and no end. One thing is certain, the business of staying alive occupies every living moment. . . . With death as a constant companion one does not have time for pettiness.

CHAPTER 10

RESCUED!

APRIL 29, 1942
Malinta Tunnel, Corregidor Island

Word came for Sally Blaine to report to the dining tunnel at sundown. She arrived with nineteen other nurses. Maude Davison told them they were relieved from duty on Corregidor and would leave for Australia by first available transport.

They gasped in disbelief.

General Wainwright had asked General MacArthur for pontoon planes to replenish

medicines and evacuate older officers, officers' wives, and nurses. MacArthur agreed to send the only two seaplanes available.

The list of nineteen ANC nurses included Rita Palmer and Rosemary Hogan, who'd been wounded in the bombing of Hospital No. 1. It also named Josie Nesbit and Ann Mealor, among the oldest nurses on The Rock, but Josie and Ann refused to go.

"I couldn't see how anybody could walk off and leave all those wounded people," Ann said.

Like Sally Blaine, a number of nurses on the list had become chronically ill. A few young nurses, however, appeared to be on the list because of their connections, one with an officer on MacArthur's staff. Maude Davison later said she'd picked the names out of a hat, but nobody believed it.

"I wanted to go, and I didn't want to go," said Juanita Redmond. "Probably I would never see the other nurses again, and I wanted to stay with them and face whatever was to come; we had faced so much together, I felt like a deserter."

Evelyn Whitlow, a friend of Sally's who was on the list, later said, "They were sending all the crazy nuts home."

"Oh, I don't think it's necessary to say that, Evelyn, please! There's enough ugly rumors without adding to it," Sally said.

The day's heavy bombing broke, and at 11:00 on the night of April 29, two seaplanes glided to a landing on the mineswept waters off Corregidor.

News spread, and friends gathered at the tunnel exit to whisper good-bye to Sally, Rita, and the others. The group arrived at the dock under a full moon, the night uncommonly quiet. Small boats carried them across the water to board the pontoon planes.

Sally, Rita, Rosemary, and Evelyn were among those who stepped aboard the first seaplane.

"Let's get going," said the pilot. "Hurry up … hurry up." The crew seemed anxious. In Australia, they had volunteered for the mission, knowing they would risk their lives.

Shortly before midnight, the engines throbbed, and the planes took off smoothly from the bay. Nurses found the fresh air exhilarating after weeks in the hot, stale tunnel, but the night was cold. The crew gave the women coats and they nestled under a blanket, leaving any worries to the pilots and crew.

The next morning the pontoon planes landed for refueling on Lake Lanao, Mindanao, one of the few Philippine Islands still in Filipino-American hands. The nurses learned that the Japanese had invaded the island that very morning and were only forty miles away. The nurses lay low that day, anxious for darkness to fall and cover their getaway.

That night they reboarded the planes. "The first plane got off, but we had trouble and hit rock, and water started coming in," Sally Blaine said. "Rosemary took off her terry-cloth jacket and stuffed it into the holes … but she couldn't keep water from coming into that plane. It got up onto the seats and over our ankles.

"I was seated next to Rita, and she said, 'Come on, Sally, let's get out of here. I'm getting off.' The general's wife pushed ahead of us and got off before we did. She forgot all about having arthritis."

In the plane's tail, water up to her waist, Evelyn Whitlow got out last.

An officer radioed for help. Another plane would be sent for them. Over the next week, the group reported to one airfield after another on the island, hoping to catch a plane. "We slept on cots, fully clothed, each night so we'd be ready to go when a plane came," said Sally.

Meanwhile, the ten Army nurses in the other seaplane arrived safely in Australia.

LEFT BEHIND ON CORREGIDOR, MADELINE Ullom asked, "Why them? Why not me? . . . We were torn. On one hand you are certain absolutely about your dedication and devotion to the patients, while on the other you wondered just how long you might withstand the trauma."

Hattie Brantley thought if she had been picked to leave, it would mean she wasn't a worthy member of the team. She was glad to stay, though nurses and soldiers alike faced increasing shortages of food and water. "Sometimes there was butter, sometimes jam, never both, often neither."

When bombs knocked out the water pumps, they had nothing to drink except canned fruit juice and saltwater. Nurses saved the fruit juice for their patients and tried to get along with saltwater boiled by the kitchen staff and flavored with coffee, lemonade, or cocoa. Alice Zwicker wrote,

> *This morning I sat down to "breakfast," which consisted of a tablespoon of cold corned beef hash on a dirty plate (no water for washing dishes) and one half glass of warm water in a dirty glass, and nothing more available until 6pm, I felt that it couldn't get worse.*

Engineers repaired the water system, but Japanese bombings hit a record on May 2. Two officers on General Jonathan Wainwright's staff counted explosions and estimated that one five-hundred-pound shell struck Corregidor every five seconds for five excruciating hours;

1.8 million pounds of explosives hit before the men stopped counting.

The shells' kick knocked down nurses and men near the tunnel entrances. Smoke and dust filled the tunnels, making the nurses' eyes water. They struggled to breathe, devising masks of gauze for themselves and their patients. The noise alone burst eardrums and impaired thought.

The next day General Wainwright radioed MacArthur. "Situation here is fast becoming desperate."

Alice Zwicker confided in her diary:

> *More and more of the patients being admitted are young kids who have simply gone haywire trying to fight bombs and shells without even rifles. But after awhile courage alone is just not enough, and something gives.*

The next night the Navy risked a daring mission. The submarine *Spearfish* stole past a Japanese minesweeper and destroyer to surface near The Rock. A small boat motored out to meet it, carrying twelve American nurses, twelve high-ranking American military officers, and one officer's wife.

The last outgoing mail was taken aboard, including some hastily scrawled letters to family. Hattie Brantley didn't bother. "I couldn't write a letter to my family. What was I going to say?"

Within an hour the *Spearfish* dove two hundred feet beneath the sea, stealing away toward Australia, leaving fifty-six Army nurses behind.

The submarine *Spearfish* on September 30, 1944, three years after her daring run through the minefields off Corregidor.

When it seemed the pounding on Corregidor could get no worse, it did. During the next twenty-four hours some sixteen thousand shells thundered down on Corregidor, an island four miles long and one mile wide. Near midnight, under a full moon, a wave of Japanese barges landed on the beach.

Nurses destroyed records and kept gas masks and helmets at the ready. Maude Davison and Josie Nesbit withdrew to contrive the best way to protect their charges.

Military strategists had first envisioned Malinta Tunnel in 1907. The gray concrete tunnel had been built secretly in the 1920s, using mining equipment and convict labor from Bilibid Prison in Manila. A crucial part of War Plan Orange, it would provide a self-sufficient fortress able to withstand siege for months.

But war planners had counted on the defenders' ability to restock supplies. No one had foreseen that an enemy might conquer the Philippine skies in two or three days, nor that the Pacific Fleet would be decimated at Pearl Harbor. The American psyche had not imagined U.S. soldiers cornered by a better-fed, better-equipped enemy outnumbering them twenty-one to one.

Even all the rumors of what the [Japanese] may do to all of us and especially the women mean little or nothing to me at the present, Alice Zwicker wrote. *Just end this awful destruction and find help for these patients who need the barest essentials so badly.*

Wainwright's troops commanded a great price from the first wave of Japanese landing barges, but the second wave reversed the score before breakfast. When enemy tanks rolled onto Corregidor's beaches, Wainwright imagined the wholesale slaughter that would befall his men, and he "thought of the havoc that even

one tank could wreak if it nosed into the tunnel, where lay our helpless wounded and their brave nurses."

Wainwright sent men out with white flags at 10:00 A.M.

Most nurses heard the news over the tunnel radio. Surrender would come at noon on May 6.

"Now our facial expressions were stony, and we avoided letting our eyes meet," said Denny Williams. "Not only our own hopeless fear, but collective fear, with its power to panic, passed from person to person like a current, lurching and jolting on-off, on-off, but always more intense until I had visions of our soldiers fighting until all were dead outside and the enemy came inside, screaming and brandishing swords and bayonets. I wondered if I would die and how I would die. I hoped to be quiet and brave."

Top: Japanese forces come ashore on Corregidor Island in the early-morning hours of May 4, 1941.

Bottom: Major Thomas Dooley (left) and General Jonathan Wainwright wait tensely for thirty minutes before Japanese Lieutenant General Masaharu Homma arrives to accept the American surrender.

CHAPTER 11
SURRENDER TO THE ENEMY

MAY 6, 1941
Corregidor Island

E ach day of the siege, a sign on the tunnel bulletin board had proclaimed: CORREGIDOR STILL STANDS. On May 6, someone mustered enough humor to amend the sign—CORREGIDOR STILL STANDS . . . UNDER NEW MANAGEMENT.

At noon outside Malinta Tunnel a bugler played taps. Two grim-faced American officers lowered the Stars and Stripes and raised a white bed sheet.

U.S. Army officers, tested by months of combat, cried like babies at news of the surrender. Doubtless the nurses cried, too. But they had a job to do, and their patients depended upon them, no matter what.

A group of U.S. Army women had never before surrendered to an enemy. Maude Davison and Josie Nesbit were determined that their nurses would uphold the highest standards of the U.S. Army Nurse Corps. Josie felt responsible for her young nurses, and she was worried.

This was the Japanese Army, which, both truly and literally, was responsible for the RAPE OF NANKING, Josie wrote later.

"I was scared spitless," said Nurse Inez McDonald.

68

Members of the Army Nurse Corps & Civilian Women who were in Malinta Tunnel when Corregidor fell

Edith Shacklett
Helen Hennessey
Jean A. Williams
Frances Nash
Oz Putman
Eunice Young
Adele Foreman
Phyllis J. Arnold
Letha McHale
Magdalena Eckmann
Minnie L. Breese
Hattie R. Brantley
Adolpha Meyer
Blanche Kimball
Gwen Henshaw
Mina Aasen
Myra V. Burris
Edith M. Corns
Madeline M. Ullom
Doris A. Kehoe
Eula Fails
Alice M. Zwicker
Clara L. Mueller

Maude C. Davison
Ann Mealer
Sallie P. Durrett
Kathryn L. Dollason
Earlyn M. Black
Beulah Greenwalt
Dorcas E. Easterling
Edith M. Wimberly
Mildred J. Dalton
Mary Ripplak
Dorothy Scholl
Helen M. Cassiani
Eleanor O. Lee
Winifred P. Madden
Ruth M. Stoltz
Dorothy Ludlow
Verna V. Henson
Mary B. Brown
Marcia Gates
Ethel Thor

Josephine M. Nesbit
Rose Rieper
Frankie Lewey
Inez V. McDonald
Mary Jo Oberst
Anne B. Wurts

CIVILIANS
Mildred Roth
Denny Williams
Ruby Motley
Brunetta A. Kuehlthau
Vivian Weisblatt
Fontaine Porter
Betty Brusfield
Catharine L. Nau
Anna Wingate
Marie Atkinson
Marcia Wolf
Rita E. Johnson

Tearing a large square from a bedsheet, the nurses scrawled at the top *Members of the Army Nurse Corps and Civilian Women Who Were in Malinta Tunnel When Corregidor Fell.* Sixty-nine women signed their names to leave a record in case they disappeared.

A nerve-racking three hours crawled by before they heard boots clomping through the passageways. The nurses jumped to their feet. A group of Japanese officers and a handful of somber-faced American officers ordered the nurses into formation. Standing at attention, they faced the wall, trying not to tremble. The women didn't move or make a sound. Some sneaked a sideways glance at their captors. Swords hung from the officers' waists, and they carried guns with bayonets. They walked up and down the line of women. They said nothing and left.

"We kept taking care of our patients," Hattie Brantley said, insisting she was not scared.

"We had discussed the possibility of rape, and it was just one of those things."

When the Japanese came to inspect the hospital, "they looked at each patient," Hattie said. "I had the traction ward, and they made sure that if everybody was in traction, they needed to be in traction. It wasn't just somebody hiding out."

Then the Japanese ordered a dozen nurses to report outside. "They lined us up out in front of the hospital tunnel, and they put an armed guard with a gun and a bayonet at each end of us," Madeline Ullom said.

An enemy officer spoke to them in excellent English. "Don't be afraid. I know how you Americans feel. I understand about you. I'm a graduate of one of your universities."

"They looked us up and down," Millie Dalton said. "They got to Blackie [Earlyn Black], tall, beautiful, from Texas. They said the next generation of Japanese would be tall. That scared her."

The Japanese snapped photos of the nurses and took down their names and next of kin. They promised to send the photos and information to General MacArthur to show that the nurses were alive and well.

General MacArthur never received the photographs, and nurses' families received the scant news that they were missing in action.

The Japanese turned off the ventilation system in Malinta, which quickly turned the tunnel into a stifling, stinking sauna. Nurses were allowed short breaks outside, where shelling and bombing had destroyed everything. Once-green lawns, flowers, lush bushes, and trees had become a wasteland of charred stumps and piles of colorless rubble and dust. The nurses sat in the sun, shooing off the swarms of flies—huge greenflies hatching in rotting flesh, for all around lay the bodies of American soldiers.

"Of course, by that time they were all swollen up terrifically. Oh, it was awful. The sights were just horrid," Madeline said. "Our officials asked repeatedly to go out and bury the dead. It was probably several days afterwards before they were buried."

A sign in Japanese was placed at the entrance of the nurses' quarters. It translated as NURSES, OFFICERS OF THE UNITED STATES ARMY. Japanese soldiers would stop to read the sign and laugh. Used to male medics, they seemed unable to believe that the nurses served in a professional capacity. In their experience, women took no part in the manly pursuit of war. Japanese soldiers paraded through at any hour of the day or night to satisfy their curiosity.

The women slept in their uniforms, and at

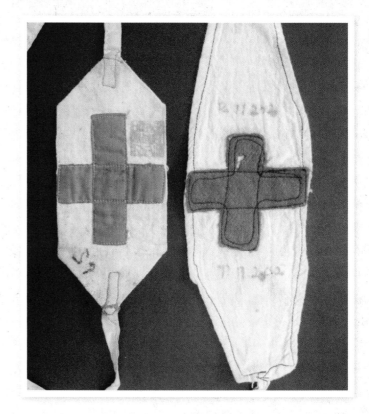

night one stood watch with a bell. When Japanese soldiers appeared, she rang the bell, and they all got up and stood at attention while the men walked through. Though the soldiers did not molest the women, they confiscated anything of value.

Once, a Japanese soldier snuck in on his own. Nurse Eleanor Garen pretended to sleep as he stole a ring right off her finger. The soldiers stole the fountain pens nurses used to keep medical records and the wristwatches they used to measure the heartbeats of their patients. Some women successfully hid jewelry in their hair along with their suicide morphine pills from the beginning of the war. Frankie Lewey saved a wristwatch by covering it with tape to make it appear old and worthless.

After two weeks, the Japanese crammed the thousands of American POW men, including hundreds of patients from the hospital, into the holds of ships bound for prison in Manila. Nurses, doctors, and corpsmen remained behind with patients who could not leave Corregidor. Only 280 sick and wounded remained of the fifteen hundred in the hospital at the time of surrender.

For the next six weeks, the hospital operated as normally as possible, but the nurses worried about what would happen to them and their patients. To boost morale, one nurse tried to organize an exercise class. She had a few takers for a short time, but the nurses were too hungry and weak to exercise, and many were sick. Frankie Lewey had developed such pain from arthritis, it was difficult for her to walk.

"I think nearly everybody had bacillary dysentery," said Madeline. "Many of the girls had malaria."

"I had developed dengue fever," Hattie Brantley said. "That's a fever that's caused by a mosquito bite. It's called breakbone fever. You feel like every bone in your body has just shattered."

On July 2 the *Lima Maru* anchored offshore, and the Japanese ordered medical equipment and patients loaded into the ship's hold, formerly used for ferrying cavalry horses. The wounded spent the night packed into the hot, airless space without food or water. Nurses slept for the last time on Corregidor in their empty hospital and boarded the ship the next morning.

Small boats took the nurses from the dock to a rope ladder dangling from the deck of the *Lima Maru*. "I did pretty good until I got about three rungs from the top," Madeline said. "I had a temperature of about 104 that day. . . . Everything started going around. I knew that the bay was full of sharks and if I fell in the water, that was the end of it." With her last ounce of strength, Madeline crawled onto the deck and lay down.

A Japanese officer served the nurses tea and cookies as the ship sailed across the bay

N.Y.K. S.S. "HAKOZAKI MARU."

Opposite: Nurses made armbands with red crosses to identify themselves as medical professionals and noncombatants.

Left: The *Lima Maru* was used to transport nurses, patients, and medical equipment across Manila Bay. The *Hakozaki Maru*, pictured here, was made by the same company and in the same design as the *Lima Maru*.

sunken ships stuck up from the fouled bay. No swaying palms surrounded the Manila Hotel, no long black limousines with chauffeurs in white linen, no splash of swimmers in the officers' club pool, no tinkle of ice in a glass, no laughter. . . .

The women forced smiles and waved as their patients in traction were carried up in nets from the hold of the freighter. They could hardly bear to watch the patients being carried onto trucks. Patients who could stand formed up military style on the dock.

Then it was the nurses' turn. Hauling their bits of baggage, American nurses were separated from the Filipino nurses and lined up on the wharf to be counted. And counted again. As doctors, corpsmen, and ambulatory patients got the signal to march, the Japanese ordered American nurses onto the beds of three waiting trucks.

"They had four armed guards on each truck with guns and bayonets," said Madeline. "We were driving along. All of a sudden I realized they weren't going out towards Paranaque, where the school was. So I decided I'd be helpful. I told them they were taking the wrong road. They didn't say anything. So I told them again. . . . They tapped me on the back with the bayonet. I decided I'd better keep still.

"Deep down we knew we would never see some of these men again. Men in whom we had vested the best treatment and care we were capable of giving, as well as our officers and doctors with whom we had worked so hard." Once again the nurses were separated from their patients. Madeline ached with sadness.

toward Manila. He told the nurses that they and their patients were going to Paranaque on the outskirts of Manila, where a school had been converted to a hospital. Finally the women relaxed, able to enjoy the slight breeze and the sight of whitecaps on the water.

"After climbing that ladder," Frances Nash said, "we should join a three-ring circus." That got a laugh. Someone brought out a grimy deck of cards, and they played a game of bridge.

In midafternoon the nurses stood at the rail as the *Lima Maru* docked. Hulks and masts of

CHAPTER 12
HELD INCOMMUNICADO

JULY 3, 1941
Santa Catalina, Manila

In the muggy afternoon three trucks rolled down España Boulevard, carrying the nurses to the University of Santo Tomas. Gray rock wall rimmed with barbed wire surrounded most of the campus. Wrought-iron fence adorned with spikes pointing skyward stretched across the front. *Sawali*, woven bamboo matting, blocked the view in and out.

Word of new American prisoners spread through the Santo Tomas Internment Camp.

Hundreds of internees—a euphemism for POWs—came running to surround the trucks entering the compound through the iron gates. To the tanned civilians clad in clean dresses and neat shorts—Allied civilians the Japanese had rounded up in Manila—the nurses must have looked a sorry sight: emaciated, in dirty, baggy coveralls, fatigued but unflinching.

The trucks pulled up in front of the main building. Internees handed up pineapples, mangos, papayas, and bananas while pelting the nurses with questions. They were desperate for some word of their husbands, fathers,

Right: Classrooms in the main building of the University of Santo Tomas campus were converted to dormitories housing approximately forty-five prisoners per room.

Opposite: Each prisoner received a meal ticket that originally entitled them to three simple meals a day, until meals dwindled to starvation rations.

brothers, and friends captured on Bataan and Corregidor.

"No talking!" the guards shouted.

In the heat of the afternoon, many of the nurses were too tired and overwhelmed to answer anyway, but Ethel Thor said they did enjoy "their first fresh fruit in six months."

As members of the armed forces, though, the nurses did not want to be imprisoned with civilians, and a few nurses decided they would demand to go to a military prison camp. Hattie Brantley spoke up. The Japanese guards shook their heads and pointed their rifles at her, motioning for the nurses to exit the truck.

"Somebody with a bayonet tells you to get off," Hattie said, "you have a tendency to get off."

Guards herded the nurses into the main building to register them, a process that took hours while the women stood waiting.

"They discussed us, shaking their heads, nodding, speaking, starting all over again," said Denny Williams, who eventually asked permission to use the bathroom. "I entered a small room with toilet stalls from which the doors had been removed. On the wall in huge letters was a printed sign: IF YOU WANT PRIVACY, CLOSE YOUR EYES."

At length, the guards came to a decision and directed the nurses outside and searched their baggage. Though spent and grieving, the women felt laughter bubble up when a soldier held up a single tampon, inspecting it from all sides. He pulled it apart, delicately, as if it might explode. The women stifled giggles. When his partner snickered and enlightened him, he dropped the tufts of cotton as if they were on fire.

Motioned back into the trucks, the nurses rode out of Santo Tomas to a convent next door, Santa Catalina, where they were given cots in a second-floor classroom. The Japanese kept the nurses isolated from the main camp and commanded they keep silent about Bataan and Corregidor.

"They wanted us to forget the atrocities and the horrible treatment . . . so that we wouldn't talk to the internees about it," Hattie said.

Night and morning the camp sent over generous amounts of fruit and vegetables, boiled meats and bread. The nurses welcomed peace and quiet and two full meals a day, but not without guilt. "We thought we should've been down taking care of the soldiers," Army Nurse Ruby Bradley said.

Several of the nurses were so sick that the Japanese allowed them to be treated at Philippine General Hospital. Over time all the nurses regained their strength. Maude Davison established military routine and discipline. Nurses exercised daily in the yard, while enemy soldiers kept watch. They answered roll call each morning.

Together in one place, the fifty-six Army nurses became unified in a way that had not been possible in the jungle or tunnel. They naturally fell into friendships old and new, and their common experience bound them tightly.

As they felt stronger, they found ways to occupy their time. Hattie learned to play bridge, making a foursome with Ethel, Frankie, and Madeline. They played for hours every day. Several nurses planted a vegetable garden in the fertile soil in the yard behind the convent. The women shared confidences, books, and any skills they possessed, whether it be sewing, singing, or fortune-telling, which made one nurse and her deck of cards quite popular. Several, including Ethel Thor, kept diaries, even

though anyone caught doing so by the guards would be punished.

After six weeks, the Japanese moved the women from Santa Catalina to the main camp at Santo Tomas. Each morning a loudspeaker woke them with a lively tune at 6:30, and they lined up to use the bathroom.

"We had three showers and five washbasins," Madeline said. "I think there were about five toilets, and that was all for the whole second floor. I suppose there must have been about three hundred people using them."

At 7:30 A.M. they joined the chow line for breakfast. Like the rest of the prisoners, they were issued an enamel plate, a cup, and a spoon. Breakfast consisted of cracked-wheat cereal, a roll, milk, and coffee. Supper was a banana, rice, mung beans, stew of some kind, maybe duck eggs or sardines.

The university had been a day school with no housing for students. The Japanese confined nearly four thousand men, women, and children to its sixty acres and three large stone

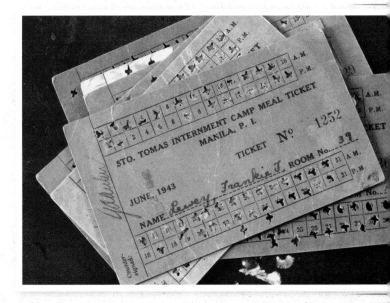

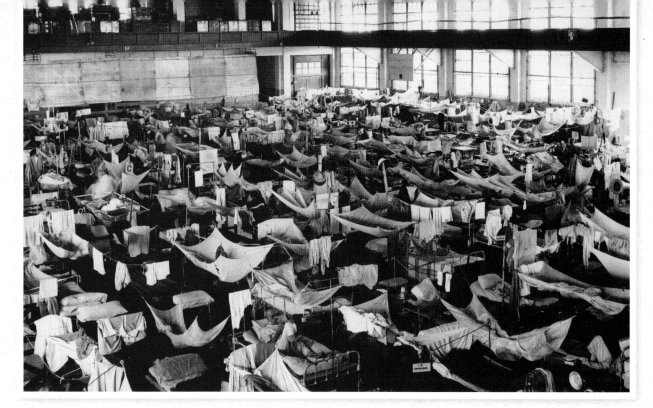

buildings. They had rounded up people from every walk of life and citizens from many countries, notably British, French, American, and Scandinavian.

The Army nurses discovered that the Japanese had incarcerated the eleven Cañacao Naval Hospital nurses in Santo Tomas back in March. Peggy Nash and the other Navy nurses had converted the university machine shop into a tiny hospital, which they staffed along with civilian doctors and other nurses who had been captured. The Navy nurses' quarters were room 30A on the second floor of the main building.

Most of the internees lived in classrooms on the second and third floors. The Japanese occupied rooms on the first floor. In addition, male internees lived in the education building and the gymnasium. Women with small children slept in an annex to the main building. A campus restaurant became the Red Cross food center.

The Army nurses were appalled by their new quarters, several second-floor classrooms in the main building, where each was allotted a space only twenty-three inches wide. Prisoners had initially slept on the concrete floors. By the time the nurses arrived, camp carpenters had secured lumber and built beds. Many internees had mattresses, blankets, and pillows, but the nurses did not.

Hattie Brantley had a bed made of wood slats. "And my mattress was a bath towel, and for years I had marks on my back from those slats."

The Executive Committee formed of prisoners governed Santo Tomas under the authority of a Japanese commandant, a bureaucrat from the Imperial Department of External Affairs. At first, the Japanese denied any responsibility for feeding the prisoners. From January 4, 1942, until July 11, the camp depended on the American Red Cross for food.

After tireless argument by the Executive Committee, the Japanese agreed in July to allocate seventy centavos daily for each prisoner. This paid for all utilities, construction, maintenance, sanitation, and medical supplies. Expenses left forty-eight centavos, or approximately twenty-four U.S. pennies, per person each day for food.

Prisoner work crews ran the kitchen and dining services under the eyes of fifty to sixty Japanese guards. They swept and mopped common areas, picked up garbage, trimmed trees, mowed lawns. Most able adults volunteered to work two hours a day to keep the camp running smoothly.

The Executive Committee assigned a number of Army nurses to clean toilets. Maude Davison immediately asked the commandant to send her women to tend to captive American soldiers instead. When he refused, Maude insisted that the Army women at least work in their professional capacities. Though a small woman, she had a commanding presence, and because the Japanese revered their elders, Maude's gray hair added to her influence.

She was assigned to take her fifty-six Army nurses and the eleven Navy nurses and organize a larger camp hospital in the Santa Catalina convent. A fenced passageway was constructed to connect the new hospital to the campus. Some of the younger Army nurses balked at working four hours a day taking care of civilians, and they challenged Maude's authority in a civilian camp. The Navy nurses also chafed under the Army commander, but Davison's resolve for the group to keep busy and help others prevailed.

Second in command to Maude, Josie Nesbit worried not only about her girls' work ethic, but about their reputations and their very sur-

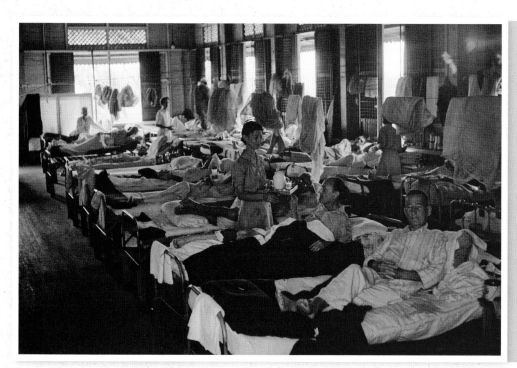

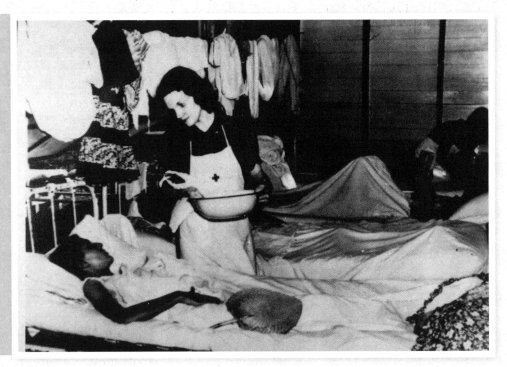

Navy Nurse Peggy Nash with a hospital patient in Santo Tomas. When Peggy was captured, her family heard nothing of her for more than a year. The Japanese unwittingly provided Nash's family with proof she was alive. This photo taken by a Japanese guard later fell into American hands and was published in U.S. newspapers, proof that the nurses were held in Japanese POW camps.

vival, which she believed would depend upon their sticking together. Her primary effort went to encouraging their pride and esprit de corps, or morale.

"We reasoned that if we hoped to remain integrated emotionally, our first and primary duty was to carry on in our most professional capacity," Josie said. "Not for one moment did we ever lose sight of the fact that not only were we prisoners of war in every sense, but also that we were U.S. Army nurses."

Navy nurses conducted themselves likewise. "I think the Japanese respected us because we were working all the time," said Peggy Nash.

The military nurses were not mistreated, beaten, or tortured in the strictest sense, but the emotional strain was intense.

A guard followed Peggy for several days before snapping her photo. She said, "We never knew what they had in mind, and we never stayed alone in a room, and kept our clothes on at all times."

In early September, the nurses were surprised by a new group of prisoners. The Japanese brought in Sally Blaine, Rita Palmer, Evelyn Whitlow, and seven other nurses who had been evacuated from Corregidor by pontoon plane. Everyone had hoped they had flown safely to Australia and then home to the States. Now here they were, ragged and weary.

The nurses made their old comrades welcome and listened to their story—how they had escaped Corregidor, only to be recaptured.

After several weeks of running and hiding from the Japanese on Mindanao, the passengers from the damaged seaplane had realized they would not be rescued. The group split up, the men joining guerrilla fighters in the hills, the nurses going to a local hospital.

When the Japanese arrived to inspect the hospital three days later, the nurses surrendered. Though prisoners, they enjoyed their brief respite from war. Filipino nurses at the hospital shared food and clothing with them. The hospital lay under a canopy of trees, and the countryside grew lush with flowers. The nurses enjoyed bathing in a pool at the bottom of a waterfall.

In late July, the Japanese loaded the nurses and captured American civilians onto a freighter bound for Manila, telling them they would be repatriated to the United States. On the way, Rita Palmer was sick with hepatitis, and Sally Blaine's dengue fever returned.

"I was very, very ill," Sally said. "After I got on the ship, I immediately unfolded my blanket, lay down, and stayed there the rest of the trip. That's when you really began to take care of me," she reminded her friend Evelyn Whitlow. "I couldn't lift my head off the pillow."

"I stood in line to get food for you, brought it back, and if you couldn't feed yourself, I fed you. Then I'd go back and get my food," Evelyn said.

"Oh, my, I didn't know that! I don't remember, because I could hardly stand up," Sally said. "You took care of me. If you hadn't, I might not be here today."

Sally did remember a Japanese medic on the ship. "He knelt down and touched my forehead and said, 'Oh, very hot!' Evelyn, you were standing near me, as you always were when I was sick. He said, 'You got ice cap? I got ice.' . . . He took you with him to get ice. When the ice melted, off you'd go to get more. He offered me medicine. I thought he was truly concerned about me, and I wasn't afraid he'd poison me. I took the medicine one or more times. Whether it helped me, I don't know."

The Japanese medic's kindness to others also touched Sally. "There was this little baby, an American child about three or four months old, left on a pallet near me while her mother went to eat. When the mother was gone, the baby started to cry. . . . The Japanese medic came by, picked the baby up, patted it a little bit, and the baby stopped crying. . . . He kissed that baby on the forehead, I'll bet a hundred times!"

"They were crazy about children," Evelyn said. "They even gave some of their food to the children!"

"He held the baby until the mother came back," Sally said. "Then he took out a billfold and showed her a picture of a baby. He told her when he had left home eight years before, he had a baby the same age as hers, but he had not seen his child since. I never did fear the Japanese much after that."

Sally and Rita spent time as patients before they were well enough to take up nursing duties with their seventy-seven Army and Navy sisters at Santo Tomas.

CHAPTER 13
SANTO TOMAS INTERNMENT CAMP

Life in Santo Tomas consisted of waiting in one line after another. The longest was the chow line, but there were also lines for washing laundry under faucets fixed over a crude trough. There were lines for the toilet, lines for showers, lines for washing hair and rinsing dishes.

Whenever Army Nurse Bertha "Charlie" Dworsky saw a line, she automatically fell in. "You knew something must be going on!"

One of the most popular lines, the package line, was set up for prisoners lucky enough to have supplies sent in from outside. Many of the internees had been businesspeople or members of wealthy families. They paid Filipino servants or friends to bring them food, clothing, household items—practically anything they wanted.

Some used this opportunity to set themselves up for business inside the camp. They sold fruit and vegetables, cookies, muffins and bread, peanuts, carabao milk, eggs, and meat. Small restaurants, coffee shops, and teahouses popped up. Even the Japanese got into the trade, selling combs, shower shoes, textiles, and thread. One enterprising woman contrived to get her beautician's chair inside the fence and did a thriving business.

The military nurses had not received paychecks in months and had no money. A long-retired U.S. Army nurse who had once worked with Josie Nesbit and Maude Davison came to their rescue. Ida Hube had married a German importer in Manila. Though her husband had died, she still had a German passport. Germany being an ally of Japan, Ida had not been interned.

Ida had come to visit the Army nurses in her huge black limousine when they first arrived at Santa Catalina. She continued to bring them food each week. Ida also delivered sanitary napkins, clothing, needles, and thread.

"She saved our lives," said Hattie.

"From time to time, a kindly soul made a loan to some of the nurses," said Josie. A little extra food made a marked difference in attitude and physical condition.

Rita Palmer, several other nurses, and a Catholic priest formed a group to look out for one another. A family of sorts, they ate together, took turns shopping and cooking, and planted vegetables.

"Our group was the envy of the whole camp when one day we ate corn off the cob grown in our own camp garden," Rita said. They had small charcoal stoves to barbecue their corn, eggplant, and other vegetables. Pooling resources, they had a table made and used a clean tablecloth at every meal. Each had a napkin embroidered with his or her name. Small niceties helped keep spirits up.

Hattie and several friends made a pact to play cribbage, gin rummy, or bridge every day, their cards soon growing grimy and tattered.

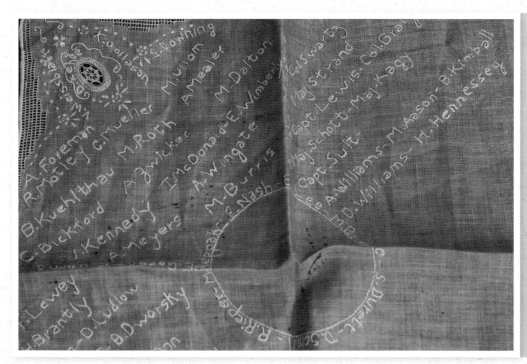

The nurses also joined activities with the civilian internees. They formed a team in the women's baseball league. They could also play basketball, soccer, and volleyball and borrow books from the library.

The internees organized school for the camp children and a wide variety of classes for adults. Language classes were popular, including Tagalog, Spanish, Hindi, Greek, Russian, French, German, Chinese, and Japanese. Rita earned the equivalent of a year's college credit, studying sociology, English literature, and logic. She resumed her childhood interest in the

violin and played in the camp's sixteen-piece orchestra.

"You could read the classics. You could listen to good music every night from seven to nine," said Hattie. "One night would be classical, and the next night would be semiclassical, and they'd have a Western night. We wrote and did plays, and we put on talk shows and entertained ourselves."

But prison is prison. "If anyone escaped, they would make a spectacle of it—bring the escapees in, beat them unmercifully, and we all had to watch," Peggy Nash said. "Their message was: Don't try to escape, because this is what's going to happen if you do."

One day Japanese soldiers dragged into camp three men who had escaped over the wall the previous day. Soldiers forced the men to dig graves and stand next to the fresh holes. Executioners' gunshots felled them into the graves.

Frances Nash, never one to hold back when she felt she was right, took chances with the Japanese. One day a guard approached her and asked for medicine for his bald spot.

"I told him I was sorry, but the Japanese would not give us any medicine," Frances said.

The guard asked where he could get some, and Frances told him, "The U.S." The doctor on duty nearly fainted at her audacity. But the guard bowed. Frances bowed. He thanked her and left.

"What's wrong?" Frances asked the doctor.

"You know there is nothing to grow hair on his bald spot," he said.

"You know he will never go to the States."

"You will get us killed, one of these days, lying to them."

"He left happy."

The doctor shook his head. They became good friends, but he never forgot her lying about the medicine for baldness.

Fenced in, elbow to elbow, people tired of being on their best behavior. Politeness couldn't hold its polish indefinitely. Within each room loud talking and snoring became unbearable, and it was aggravated by bedbugs, mosquitoes, ants, flies, and lice. Nurses had only a few inches of personal space, with beds so close that they could barely walk between them.

They grasped any reason to celebrate. Rita's group remembered the birthdays and anniversaries of their families far away in the States, baking a cake in a clay oven and spreading a special tablecloth.

As Christmas 1942 approached, the women made simple gifts for one another, but the best gifts were the comfort kits delivered by the Red Cross. Each internee received small cans of meat spread, bacon, condensed milk, margarine, marmalade, pudding, tomatoes, cheese, soda crackers, tea, sugar, a piece of chocolate, and a small bar of soap.

The camp orchestra, with Rita on violin, played a Christmas concert featuring Handel's *Messiah*. U.S. Army Engineer POWs kept on Corregidor to work for the Japanese managed to send money to the nurses, which they used to have a Christmas party with cake and ice cream.

Still, the nurses suffered demoralizing bore-

dom, or, as Denny Williams called it, "great mental and emotional fatigue born of idle hours and inane conversations."

"All day it was a question of keeping body and soul together," said Hattie Brantley. "When you washed your clothing, you went out and laid it on the grass. There were no such things as clotheslines. You sat by while it dried because somebody could steal it if you looked the other way. And by the time you filled your day with four hours of duty and washed your clothes and dried them and did a few things for yourself and read a good book, the day was gone."

While some civilian internees angered the nurses by treating them like servants, Sascha Weinzheimer, an eleven-year-old American girl, was grateful for their care when she spent two weeks in the hospital recovering from a tonsillectomy. A raging infection and malnutrition impeded Sascha's healing, and Denny sat with her through the nights, calling the doctor whenever Sascha's throat started to bleed.

"It was hard to remember they were also

prisoners," Sascha said of the Army nurses. "We looked at them like saviors. . . . They were absolutely amazing women."

Back home in the States, nurses' families heard nothing of them after the surrender of Corregidor. The War Department classified them as missing in action (MIA), and next of kin received a letter from the War Department:

. . . was serving in the Philippines at the time of the final surrender.

In the last days before the surrender of Bataan there were casualties which were not reported to the War Department. Conceivably the same is true of the surrender of Corregidor. . . . The Japanese government has indicated its intention of conforming to the terms of the Geneva Convention with respect to the interchange of information regarding prisoners of war. At some future date this Government will receive through Geneva a list of persons who have been taken prisoners of war. Until that time the War Department cannot give you positive information.

Ethel Thor's sister Vivian received slightly more comfort from a letter she was sent from one of the nurses evacuated from Corregidor.

Your sister, Ethel, handed me this address on April 29 when I was leaving Corregidor. At that time she was working very hard but was in good spirits.

She is one of my best friends, and I only wish I could give you a more recent report of everything . . . please try not to worry—I know it's impossible, for my husband is still there, but really those girls are in a group, and the medical detachment will be useful to the [Japanese], and there will be plenty of work for them to do. . . . You have been notified that Ethel is missing. I feel sure that she is no more missing than the other fifty nurses left there.

Ethel will be all right—you can bet on that. She has more friends than any of the kids, and as long as there is work to do, she doesn't grumble.

In January 1943 internees in Santo Tomas numbered 3,263, but the Japanese continued to bring in more, many of them American and British missionaries from rural areas and the outer islands. By May the census was 4,200. The Japanese decided to open another camp at Los Baños, the grounds of an agriculture college southwest of Manila. They planned to eventually move all Santo Tomas internees there but started by asking for eight hundred young, healthy male volunteers. The eleven Navy nurses, wanting some distance from Army authority, volunteered to go and provide nursing care.

MAY 14, 1943
Los Baños, Luzon, Philippines

PEGGY NASH WOKE BEFORE DAWN AND packed for the move to Los Baños. Nurses stood for roll call with the eight hundred men who would set up the camp for the eventual ten thousand prisoners the Japanese anticipated.

The women piled into the last of twelve trucks lined up to leave. A crowd gathered, cheering and waving good-bye. Peggy found it suddenly frightening to be leaving. She clutched her duck egg and piece of bread allotted for the journey. As the trucks rolled out of the gate, the camp band started to play "Anchors Away."

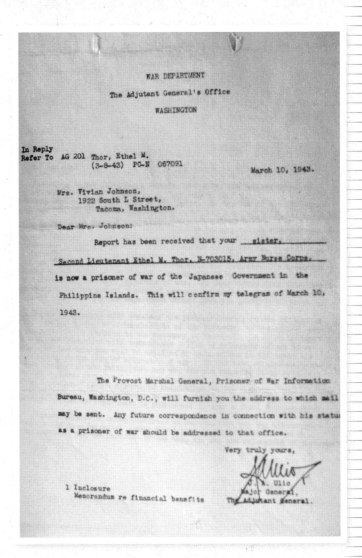

"I must be allergic to something," mumbled one nurse, wiping her eyes. Everyone else must have been, too. "We were all crying," said Peggy.

Shortly after, the trucks arrived at the railroad station, and Peggy was shocked to see a string of boxcars on the platform. "I thought, surely they're not going to put us in a boxcar."

Yes, they were—sixty to a car that might have comfortably held thirty. Guards assigned the nurses two or three to each car. They reached their destination after more than six hours crammed in the hot boxes. Nurses rode the final two miles to Los Baños in the back of a truck, while the men followed at a march.

Refreshed by the countryside, they gulped the clean air and noticed wildflowers and birdsong. Los Baños lay near the southern shore of Laguna de Bay, the Philippines' largest lake. A barbed-wire fence surrounded their new home, but it was beautiful and tranquil compared to Santo Tomas. The nurses unpacked in the one dormitory. The men would sleep in the gymnasium until they turned stacks of lumber, sections of palm roofing, and rolls of *sawali* into barracks. The pink stucco infirmary sat on the main road, backed by a little stream that ran through the camp.

Peggy and the other nurses scrubbed and swept and made do. The infirmary had been looted of almost everything. A portable instrument sterilizer looked as if it had shorted out when someone cooked rice in it. The Japanese came up with an assortment of surgical instruments and an old operating table. As soon as the twenty-five-bed hospital opened, internees arrived for treatment.

The Japanese billed Los Baños as a health resort where internees could grow vegetable gardens in fertile soil and raise animals to provide meat for their diet. It wasn't as good as promised, but the nurses were happy they had come. They planted gardens and took shifts in the hospital. Brahms's "Lullaby" played on the loudspeaker to end the day.

But they knew that family and friends worried about them. They longed for the war to end. They wanted to go home.

"It was, day after day, the same routine: jungle rot, funguses, the diarrhea, dengue fever, and malaria," said Peggy. "It was typical to have fifteen men in my dispensary soaking their feet in . . . whatever we had."

When the internees had finished building rough dormitory-style housing, more people transferred in from Santo Tomas, and soon the tranquil atmosphere disappeared. In December 1943 the second large group, many women and children, arrived with twelve boxcars loaded with possessions. Immediately Los Baños's flourishing garden produce was divvied into smaller portions.

The nurses' dormitory rooms were soon needed to expand the hospital. They squeezed into cramped quarters, chafing one another's nerves. Their uniforms wore out, and they ripped apart the sailors' jeans they had been given when the war started and used the fabric to sew new uniforms. Any resemblance to a health resort was gone.

Opposite: **Volunteers in the camp kitchen stir pots of watery vegetable-rice gruel.**

1943–1944
Santo Tomas Internment Camp

Early on, Army nurses hoped to be freed from Santo Tomas within months. Gradually, they realized they might be prisoners for years.

At first, internees laughed at others who planted banana and papaya trees, which wouldn't produce for a year. Later, no one smiled when a man dared plant an avocado tree, which would take seven years to bear fruit.

The effects of captivity grew more ominous in the fall of 1943. Nurses lost energy because they hadn't enough to eat. Millie Dalton got scurvy, which causes fatigue and swollen gums, resulting in loose teeth. Everyone's clothing and shoes wore out.

"Bakis were worn for shoes," said Rita Palmer. "These were wooden soles tied with hemp straps to hold them to the feet."

Millie was lucky to snag a pair of men's oxfords. "When your underwear wears out, you're just lost," she said. "Captain Davison got ahold of some sheets and gave each one of us a sheet. Well, I didn't need a sheet, but I needed

The Japanese soldiers did not physically abuse the nurses, but their constant presence, always watching, caused great mental strain and felt dehumanizing.

underwear. I cut up my old bras for a pattern and made myself new bras, put the old hooks and eyes on them."

One of the men made bamboo knitting needles for the nurses. Ida Hube brought them twine used in better days to tie grocery packages. The nurses used it to knit socks, panties, and bras, passing around handwritten knitting patterns. Hattie Brantley took pride in learning to turn the heel of a sock as well as her grandmother had.

Red Cross comfort kits came in December 1943, but Japanese inspectors first tore them open, slashed boxes, and stabbed cans of salmon and meat with their knives. While hungry people stood by, helpless, ants swarmed packets of raisins and prunes dropped on the ground in the hot sun. Some food spoiled, but what was left was handed out later that afternoon. Each nurse cherished her share and prudently conserved it.

Everyone found it grim to celebrate their third Christmas in Santo Tomas. Dinner and gifts provided by Ida Hube cheered the nurses. Surely by next Christmas, they reassured one another, they would be home.

In February 1944, everyone in camp gathered for a speech by the Japanese commandant. He confessed he had initially resented Americans for their arrogance, but his feelings had changed to appreciation. "I have found that at heart you are just the same as the Japanese," he said.

Then he warned the prisoners that the benevolence of the Japanese Army had limits. "We can afford generosity because we are victorious," he said.

Then he was gone. The Japanese military took control of Santo Tomas, changing its name to Prison Camp No. 1. The new commandant isolated prisoners from the outside world, stopping the package line and incoming newspapers. Nurses no longer got groceries delivered by Ida Hube in her black limousine. The chronically ill, who had been allowed out on special passes to ease crowding at the camp, were ordered back. The new regime also cut off supplies of medicine, vitamins, blood plasma, medical instruments, and equipment for surgery.

Nurses had more patients and fewer ways to treat them. In addition, epidemics swept the camp—chicken pox, whooping cough, measles, diphtheria—and depression and anxiety increased. A prisoner arrived at the hospital after she tried to leap from a third-story window; another attempted to end her life by drinking iodine.

The gloom lifted briefly when the Japanese distributed mail delivered by the Red Cross, the first news some captives had had from their loved ones in two years. People ripped open parcels and letters from home, greedily taking in the contents. Guards permitted them to write back—one letter, twenty-five words or less.

Then the military commandant notified the Executive Committee it would no longer be given money to buy food for the camp. The Imperial Army would provide food, the commandant promised. The diet became mostly mung beans and rice. Nurses dreamed of meat. Milk and bread supplies dropped by half. Sugar was rationed. Hunger became relentless, and worms and weevils never failed to appear for meals.

The Executive Committee requested more food.

"If you want more food, grow it yourselves," the Japanese replied. "You need to realize there is a great war going on. People all over the world are suffering. Every man, woman, and child should have a garden."

This sounded plausible, but Santo Tomas had no tools and no seeds. "It was like making bricks without straw, but we used knives, pieces of pipe, and sticks," said Eva Nixon, an American missionary. "We planted talinum, a spinach-like plant that grew in four to six weeks. One day the Japanese allowed a carabao to come in, and men broke ground with an antiquated plow."

Nurses had been able to borrow money from others in camp who trusted they would repay the debt at the end of the war. But what little food remained in camp now sold for outrageous prices. Those who could afford it bought it up.

"It took every bit of willpower to learn to accept what was inevitable," said Josie Nesbit. "They were not going to share with us—and that was that."

Millie Dalton was a fortunate exception. "I knew a Dutch banker who was in and out of the hospital a lot. One morning he asked me if I could cook. And I said, 'Well, I'll sure try.' He said, 'I have some canned things I will share with you if you'll cook for me.' So at lunchtime I would go with him to his shanty. We'd cook rice, and he had some canned meats and canned butter. . . . He had a footlocker full. . . . and we'd put a teaspoon of that in the rice," Millie said.

Soon, however, even the rich joined the poor in eating camp food, and the lines grew longer than ever.

Of all emotions mental, and of all feelings physical, HUNGER is unquestionably the most overpowering! Josie Nesbit wrote later. *I assure you, when you are hungry, you will do almost anything. Anything.*

Josie's mother-bear instincts rose to a new height. She gathered her older nurses to help encourage the younger women and remind them of their duty to country and one another. Later Josie wrote, *Our Junior Nurses were (pardon my frankness) literally "sitting on a gold mine" insofar as personal needs and wants were concerned. Anyone of the sixty-eight could have defected to the enemy if only to make her life easier. NONE DID! Anyone could have sold "favors" for extra money and/or food. NONE DID!*

Each passing month brought more deprivation. Millie had a wisdom tooth pulled with little anesthetic. Rations of rice and corn dwindled, and the main food became *camotes,* a poor-quality sweet potato grown in the Philippines. Even the healthiest prisoners suffered malnutrition. The number of calories allotted to each prisoner dropped from 1,490 a day to 1,180, about half the average adult requirement.

In July the commandant stopped all organized entertainment. Classes ended as teachers and students grew too malnourished to concentrate. The baseball league canceled its season. Women no longer had the strength to lift a bat or the energy to run.

The nurses could hardly remember their former lives when they had dressed up and gone dancing. Under Josie Nesbit's watchful eye many of the young nurses dated men they met in camp, but it took extraordinary effort to keep up their appearances.

Sally Blaine had suffered twenty bouts of malaria and had surgery for intestinal problems caused by poor diet. She was skin and bones. Yet every morning before leaving her room, she curled her hair with rag rollers, brushed her teeth with hand soap, and made up her face using a precious lipstick and a lead pencil.

"We traded lots of things. I traded baking soda for fingernail polish," said Sally. "One time I walked over to my friend Jimmy Horton's shanty after I'd just taken a bath and made up my face as best I could. He looked at me and said, 'Well, Sally, you look awful cute, but a ham sandwich would look better.'"

Any kind of sandwich was wishful thinking. By August there was no bread to be had, and the Japanese provided less than one ounce of meat and fish per person each day. Stealing became rampant. In mid-September the rice ration was cut from fifteen ounces to ten and a half ounces per person, per day. The commandant blamed transportation difficulties. A week later each prisoner's portion of rice decreased by another ounce and a half. The Executive Committee doled out forty extra grams of rice for each person from camp reserves.

"Occasionally they could add vegetables the prisoners grew for themselves on tiny plots of ground inside the camp," said Madeline Ullom. She had waited months on a list to be assigned a small garden, where she grew mung beans.

The consequences of this slow starvation became obvious. Nurses recognized the symptoms of beriberi. Lumps showed under the skin. Hands and feet became swollen, and people had difficulty walking as their extremities lost feeling.

The children in the camp fared slightly better. The kids hung around when the soldiers were eating until the men couldn't stand it anymore. "They would toss scraps of food from the table to the wide-eyed, hungry children," Rita Palmer said.

When everyone is hungry, nothing is more important than equal shares. Camp leaders standardized serving scoops and posted guards over the pots of rice or mush. The server dipped the ladle in, leveled it off, scraped away any food hanging from the sides, then scraped the inside of the scoop clean to assure that all got their fair share. Internees passed a law forbidding anyone to lick an empty serving pot. Kitchen workers rinsed pots with water and saved the water for the next soup.

Burned rice that stuck to the bottom of a pan had once been thrown away. When people began to line up around the building to grab it, leaders ruled that the burned rice would now be ground up and used in soup. Even weeds became precious and could only be used by the camp kitchen. One internee served a fifteen-day jail sentence under the stairs for picking some pigweed for his own private use.

Rita Palmer saved her coffee grounds, dried them under her bed, and used them over and over until the "coffee" was merely colored water. As soup and rice gradually became more and more watery, Rita's group tried to vary the taste, discovering that a bit of baking soda improved sour rice. One day they used carefully hoarded cold cream to fry the rice.

"It was surprising how well it tasted," Rita said.

When fuel for the kitchen cook fires ran out, the camp cut down the beautiful acacia trees and burned university furniture. There were personal shortages, as well. Toilet paper had been doled out to room monitors each morning. Rita's room "delegated a girl we named Miss Issue Tissue to give us our precious four or five sheets. Otherwise we shared medical-supply wrappings, the *Tribune*, or any scrap of paper we could find." Now the commandant's office announced there was no toilet paper left in the Philippines.

Food, however, remained uppermost in people's minds. If they couldn't eat it, they could think about it, dream about it, and talk about it. The person with a magazine showing pictures of food had to fight off new friends. People pushed and shoved trying to gaze for a moment on a picture of chocolate cake.

Sally Blaine found a recipe in a novel. "It had potatoes and peas and carrots and a little bit of beef or lamb, and it sounded so delicious that I read the recipe over and over again."

"A strange kind of madness swept the camp," Frances Nash said.

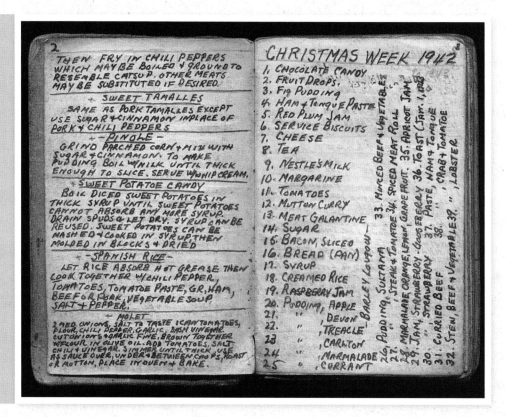

Recipe madness.

Any time of the day, up and down the halls, men and women with pencils and scraps of paper in hand could be heard saying the likes of "You take half a pound of butter, add sugar, eggs, chocolate, cream, nuts . . . chill and serve." Young and old, men and women, traded recipes and stuffed them into bulging notebooks. The nurses were not immune. Nurse Anna Williams had fantastic recipes, because she collected a great variety from the many different ethnic groups in the camp.

An internee doctor said to her patient, "Do you not realize that this recipe copying is one of the signs of insanity from malnutrition?" A week later the doctor was trading recipes, too. "I know it's silly," she said, "but it's fun."

The morning of September 21, the prisoners paid little attention to the buzzing of fighter jets in the distance. They'd become used to the sight of Japanese Zeros in the skies over Manila. Nurses on duty in the hospital went on with their routines, and people outside didn't waste the strength to lift their heads. The thrumming jet engines grew louder and broke through the clouds over Santo Tomas.

Denny Williams looked up and saw not the Japanese red sun, but wings with white stars in blue circles. "I couldn't believe it until enemy guns opened fire."

CHAPTER 15
HOPE AT LAST

SEPTEMBER–OCTOBER 1944
Santo Tomas Internment Camp

"They're Americans!" someone yelled. Then came a chorus of shouts: "Our planes! Our planes! Ours!"

Prisoners suddenly found energy. Wild with joy, they rushed outside. Nurses hugged and kissed. One counted seven American planes. People jumped up and down and cheered.

The guards ordered everyone inside, saying they would punish anyone who looked up at the planes.

The American raid lasted two hours. Nurses peered out windows at columns of smoke rising above the Manila docks. U.S. fighters flashed back and forth above the city. They hit a large Japanese cargo plane, knocking it to the ground.

That afternoon American bombers flew a second raid over Manila. Keeping back from the windows or looking through peepholes, people shouted, "Look at that one dive! See that bomb dropping! Listen! Isn't it beautiful?" Hope soared. The Americans had returned to liberate them!

As the Japanese cut back on rations, the Executive Committee had held back reserves in case things got worse. Now the camp celebrated with double portions for supper—two scoops of rice, plus a few vegetables and meat.

In the coming days two hundred more Imperial Army soldiers marched in and strutted about the campus with fixed bayonets. They ran combat drills. They forced work gangs of prisoners weakened by hunger to build guard shacks and to clear a zone next to the outside wall and string barbed wire.

Guards showed up in the dormitory day or night without warning to paw through people's belongings. They never found a radio that was hidden in the camp, which broadcast news of American victories moving across the Pacific, island by island.

Informal counts of the population by room monitors gave way to strict military routines. Each morning and night internees stood in formation, sometimes for as long as two hours. Once, guards called roll four times in one day.

"They'd wake us up at two in the morning. . . . We'd stand in the corridor and wait for four thousand people to be counted," Millie Dalton said. She tried to take it in stride. "There's no use worrying about it . . . because they would take people out, and they would never show up again. Mostly men, they never took out any

94

women, but you never knew from one day to the next what would happen to you."

"We would have to stand with one foot on one step, and one on the other, if that's where we were when the search started," Madeline Ullom said. "We'd be that way for hours." In their weakened state, these roll calls and searches became endurance tests for the nurses.

The wait for rescue became excruciating. Every night the camp was blacked out. Air raids became more frequent. But as U.S. forces fought closer, the prisoners' food decreased still more. People began to die of starvation-related diseases.

"It may have been that the Japanese did not have it for themselves," Rita Palmer said. "Some people became panic-stricken and ate boiled hibiscus leaves or cats. . . . The large flock of pigeons that had nested in the eaves gradually disappeared."

In early October the International YMCA donated a flock of ducks to the internees. The meat was ground and mixed into fried rice. A blackboard announced the day's menu:

Two hundred ducks—293 lbs. gross, 190 lbs. net; the ducks were starving, too.

By October 15, each prisoner received only about six ounces of food a day, two ounces of mush for breakfast, two ounces of rice for lunch, and two ounces of rice with gravy for supper.

Those who could find them dug canna bulbs to eat. Banana trees were cut down and the stalks cooked. All cats disappeared. Rat control had been shut down earlier in the year, and now the rats proliferated. A man dared to

Opposite: American and Filipino civilians prepare lunch in a courtyard at Santo Tomas. Prisoners often had to use their ingenuity to stretch meals.

Above: A mother feeds her children at Santo Tomas.

cook the first rat, and others followed. Women with families threw away their pride and looted the Japanese garbage cans. Children cried for food, begged, and stole. Seeing the children starving was the hardest to bear for many of the nurses. They watched fathers die of starvation after repeatedly giving their own food to their children.

1944
Los Baños Internment Camp

THE LOS BAÑOS INTERNMENT CAMP HAD grown to 1,600 prisoners. The hospital expanded again, and the Navy nurses were mentally and physically exhausted. Water was turned on only two hours a day. Gardening became an absolute necessity as rations decreased.

If only the corn grew as fast as the greens, thought Peggy Nash. She had been a tall, thin, 130 pounds when the war started. On the Los Baños diet, she fell to eighty pounds. For breakfast she ate *lugao*, a mush that tasted like "wallpaper paste" and had weevils in it. "They would give us milk for it, and if you were lucky, you'd get a banana," said Peggy. "The second of our two meals a day was a stew of all native vegetables, and that was served at 5:00 P.M. We had no meat, no protein of any kind."

A garrison of Japanese soldiers moved in, and another four hundred civilians. The camp gardens could not feed everyone. Inmates started eating leaves and even digging up loathsome slugs for food. "We'd look outside the fence and see monkeys in the banana trees," Peggy said. "We'd see them peel bananas. We stared at them. We were really starving." Guards shot any prisoner caught going over the fence.

The hospital filled with patients suffering malnutrition, and then the deaths began.

When Peggy's legs and arms puffed with fluid, she knew she had the dreaded beriberi. Weak and short of breath, with a temperature of 106 degrees, she soon lay in one of her own hospital beds.

Over time, Peggy recovered enough to get back on her feet. "We kept taking care of patients, though we were all getting weaker. I was getting to the point where I'd look at a pair of steps and think, I can't walk up, and neither could anyone else. You never knew when you went to bed at night, if you'd wake up.

"How many died, I'll never know. Two or three died every day. One would say to another, 'If you think you're going to die, you better start digging your grave, because I am just too weak.'"

Navy nurses joked with people, trying to keep up spirits. When one woman cried, afraid she was dying, Peggy evoked a smile, telling her, "You can't die. We can't bury you here; you don't have any nice clothes to put on."

Faith in God, family, and the nursing profession helped Peggy Nash keep hope alive. She said, "We kept busy . . . we didn't have time to think about ourselves."

Opposite: Santo Tomas prisoners Anthony Bernard Vlasate and Violet Wuelper Vlasate.

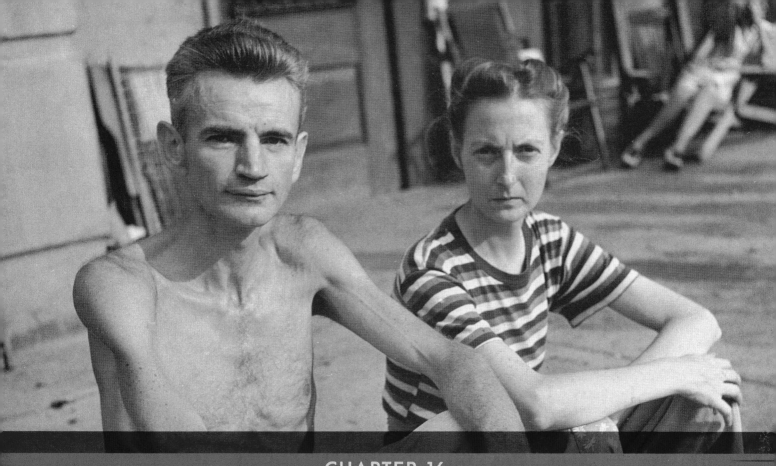

CHAPTER 16

WALKING SKELETONS

NOVEMBER 1944
Santo Tomas Internment Camp

Liberators were coming. They must be. Why else would the Japanese at Santo Tomas go on the defense? More Japanese troops arrived and dug in at Santo Tomas, using the camp to shield themselves from American bombing raids. As the Japanese suffered more losses in the war, Japanese soldiers in Santo Tomas became consumed with the need for prisoners to demonstrate proper respect. Teachers came in to give everyone three days of instruction and practice in the art of bowing.

Nodding the head would not do. Everyone must bend at the waist, lowering the entire upper body. Improper bowing became a criminal offense. Some soldiers would smile and turn away, so a bow wasn't required. Others insisted on perfection, forcing people to bow as many as seven times before being allowed to pass. Nurses had become so weak, they worried that when they bent over, they might topple to the ground.

"We had to laugh or cry," Madeline Ullom

said, "and we weren't going to let the Japanese see us cry."

Thanksgiving dinner was one scoop of rice with vegetable stew and a small serving of *camote* tops. Every day now, patients died. The nurses could only try to make patients comfortable. Many were beyond saving, even if help came.

Josie Nesbit's decades of professional objectivity did not prepare her to helplessly watch her nurses' failing health. Some had lost more than forty pounds. Josie noticed, "Their eyes gradually sank deeper into hollowed cheekbones. Their gait slowed down more and more as their strength grew less; even their shoulders drooped."

Eighty percent of the internees suffered symptoms of beriberi in varying stages, and nurses did, too. Many had intestinal ailments. Lack of protein caused incontinence.

"I'd wake up in the morning, and when I'd stand up, I'd start urinating on myself," said Sally Blaine. "It was absolutely so embarrassing, it was terrible. Some of the girls really flooded themselves in front of other people."

Josie paid the Executive Committee a visit. "We've got to have more meat for these girls," she said. The committee was able to ration an extra ounce or two of meat per week for each nurse to help them continue to care for the sick and dying.

Hunger stripped feelings raw. People didn't have the strength to "make nice." Sally Blaine lost her temper with the nurse who slept next to her. "Every night she'd come and ask me after the lights were out, 'Sally, are you hungry? Wouldn't a steak taste good? Would you like to have some chocolate pie?' And I'd say, 'Oh, be quiet! Please don't talk about it.'"

On December 23, a platoon of Imperial Japanese military police, the terrifying Kempeitai, marched into Santo Tomas. They searched the camp and with no explanation arrested four members of the Executive Committee. Punishment for minor infractions became more brutal. The Kempeitai brought American POW soldiers who'd been tortured into the camp hospital. When they recovered, the Kempeitai hauled them out again for more questioning.

The Warriors of FREEDOM Have Landed!

LEAFLETS DROPPED TO FILIPINOS

Patriots of the Philippines :—

American and Philippine forces are liberating your country from Japanese oppression. Enemy air, land and sea forces have already suffered heavy reverses in the Leyte area.

As our landings continue, it is essential that our bombers and fleet prepare the way.

We do not want to injure a single Filipino. During the period from the 15th of December to the 8th of January follow these instructions carefully :—

Stay away from the Japanese troops and any place where they are gathered together.

Avoid all buildings, dumps, airstrips, and bridges used by the Japanese.

And most important of all, at the first sign of our landing, move away from the beaches. Move inland as far as possible.

For your own safety comply with this request.

Opposite: The Kempeitai officers who arrived at Santo Tomas would have worn a uniform that looked like this. They were similar to German secret police, the Schutzstaffel (SS), and maintained public order within Japan and occupied territories.

Above: A U.S. leaflet dropped on the Philippines on January 7, 1945.

Frances Nash helped care for one man when he returned. That night she had a nightmare and woke up her roommates screaming, "No, no, don't beat him! Don't beat him again!" Tears ran down her cheeks as she described the bruises on the man's body, the festering sores, and the chafed and infected skin on his wrists from tight bindings.

The larger conflict of the war unfolded in the skies above. Nurses saw planes shot in the air, planes crash in the city, and bombs explode. When a bomb dropped, sending a huge column of smoke shooting upward, many Americans would cheer. When an American plane spun in the sky and fell in flames, Japanese soldiers clapped and shouted. They acted like spectators at a sporting event, but everyone knew the game had deadly consequences. And their own lives depended on the final score.

On Christmas Eve, American planes dropped leaflets into Santo Tomas.

The Commander-in-Chief, the officers and the men of the American Forces of Liberation in the Pacific wish their gallant allies, the people of the Philippines, all the blessings of Christmas and the realization of their fervent hopes for the New Year.

American B-24 Liberators bomb Cavite, January 24, 1945. Cavite was the former naval base of the U.S. Asiatic Fleet destroyed by the Japanese in December 1941.

The guards ordered that leaflets found in camp be turned over immediately. Anyone discovered in possession of one was jailed for seven days.

Christmas came in a teaspoonful of jam and a bite of chocolate for each prisoner, and for supper, fried rice.

After Christmas Santo Tomas fell into a state of despondency. Six or seven people died every day. Not enough healthy people remained to do chores. Garbage and human waste accumulated in the stairs and halls. On New Year's Day, a Japanese officer was heard to say that restricted diet and disease would take care of the Santo Tomas population in due course. Five days later, a number of internees saw the Kempeitai haul the Executive Committee men from the camp jail and disappear through the gates with them.

The next day the Japanese burned records under thundering skies as U.S. air raids ramped up. Again, the soldiers ordered the internees not to watch the planes, "but it was impossible to keep one's eyes off the tragic drama of war . . . wings were constantly overhead, constant explosions, constant searches of the camp by

Japanese officers. Constant terror and death," Eva Nixon said.

The night ten people died in the tuberculosis ward, Evelyn Whitlow asked to be relieved of duty. "I couldn't stand it anymore," she said. "They were coughing up blood on me, and the dead were out in the hallway wrapped up in sheets."

Japanese army officials announced the dead would no longer be taken outside the camp for burial. The bodies were supposed to be collected and buried in mass graves inside the walls.

"The people were dying, and we were having to keep their bodies in the hospital," said Madeline Ullom. "There were loads and loads of rats; some of them were a foot long, and some of them were bigger, and that's not counting their tails. . . . The rats were eating the fingers and toes off the bodies."

The commandant demanded that the camp doctors remove the words *starvation* and *malnutrition* from death certificates. The chief physician refused, and a soldier marched him off to jail.

The days of January marked either a slow death or a weakening grasp on life. Prisoners cut activity to a minimum. Saving strength might keep a body alive one more day, and that might be the day rescue would come.

Rita Palmer became so weak with dysentery and hunger that she was hospitalized, as she had been on Corregidor. This time, she feared she was dying. At 5'6", she weighed only eighty pounds.

Madeline, at 5'2", dropped forty pounds, and her teeth were falling out. She suffered from dysentery, beriberi, and scurvy. Denny Williams lost sixty-one pounds.

At the end of January, the nurses received only five hundred calories a day, usually one cup of watery vegetable gruel with moldy rice.

Frances Nash was tormented when "people would come up to me crying and begging and asking what to do about getting more food." The prisoners appeared like walking skeletons with pipe-stem legs, scarcely able to bear the bodies above them.

By February, the Japanese were hungry, too. They stripped any remaining fruits and vegetables from the prisoners' gardens.

"We had stood more than I had ever thought the human body and mind could endure," said Frances. On her way to some task, she found herself standing absolutely still, staring into space.

"There were times when my mind could not recall . . . when I had lived as anything but a prisoner," Frances said. "It was easier to remember my childhood than the year before the war. . . . There was nothing beautiful in our lives except the sunsets and the moonlight. I would sit at the window for hours, dreaming of home."

Amid bomb blasts and antiaircraft fire, the billows of thick smoke and fires blazing in the dark beyond Santo Tomas's gates, some of the nurses had a bet going. Who would arrive first? The Cavalry, the Marines, or the vultures?

Scores of internees seemed to have conceded to the vultures, lying in their beds day

In October 1944, U.S. forces land on Leyte Island, the first stop in retaking the Philippines. News of this arrived at Santo Tomas on a contraband radio hidden by internees, announced via a popular American song, "Better Late than Never." The Japanese were oblivious to a significant mispronunciation in the title: *Leyte*, pronounced "Lay-tee," was substituted for *Late*.

Opposite: The first American flag to hang in Santo Tomas in three years. February 4, 1945.

and night. Others had to feed, wash, and dress them. Water pressure failed on the second and third floors of the main building. Waiting for a turn at the first-floor toilets was an eternity for those who had the strength to get in line. Only the continued flyovers by U.S. planes offered incentive to wake up one more day.

Soldiers had rolled barrels under the central staircase in the main building. What was in them? everyone wondered. Dynamite? Gasoline? Would the Japanese burn the camp and destroy them all? Hearing the whispered rumors, Frankie Lewey barely cared. Her joints ached so much she could hardly stand. Her stomach seemed to rub against her backbone. Her once-thick red hair felt like faded straw. And she was so tired.

CHAPTER 17
LIBERATION!

FEBRUARY 3, 1945
Santo Tomas Internment Camp

A glorious sunset dazzled the camp on February 3. A formation of eight U.S. Marine Corps bombers flew so low over the prison, people saw the pilots grinning. Adults and children screamed and waved. The pilots dipped their wings. One of them tossed something down. A mad dash ensued for the pair of goggles. A note was attached.

Roll out the barrel, Christmas will be either today or tomorrow.

The message swept through the camp. Frankie Lewey heard it within minutes. Could it be true?

The Japanese guards shouted. Nervous and irritable, they ordered everyone to their quarters. A voice announced over the loudspeaker that anyone looking out a window would be shot.

Dusk fell. Gunfire sounded in the distance. Army nurses sat in their rooms talking. It was hard to imagine being free . . . going home. The only thing that took shape in their minds was what kind of food liberators might bring.

Frankie's last meal had been a bit of moldy rice twelve hours before.

Another burst of gunfire. This one closer. Wasn't it? They stood back, out of view, near the second-floor windows of the main building. Fires burned across the city.

Without warning the electricity cut out, and the campus was plunged into darkness. Japanese voices, excited and shrill, pierced the dark. Rifle and machine-gun fire popped. Loud. Close.

Flares shot into the sky outside the front gate. Frankie stared into the darkness, her heart beating wildly. The nurses clutched one another with desperate, bony fingers. A rumbling—a mechanical, earthshaking growl—filled their ears. The smell of gasoline . . . a sudden glaring light . . . a thundering crash . . . a rolling shudder. Down went the front gate.

Friend or enemy?

A mechanical monster smashed through. A powerful searchlight beamed from the armored tank grinding straight toward them, stopping just shy of the front doors.

Shadowy figures dismounted.

"Hello, folks!" The voice was unmistakably American.

Screaming, shouting, crying prisoners leaned from the windows. Inside the building, people went berserk with joy, stumbling down the stairs, spilling into the plaza. Some prisoners fainted to the dirt; others prayed, hugged, and kissed; and others mobbed the soldiers.

Someone in the crowd started to sing "God Bless America." A thousand voices joined in, and the song rose and swelled. The red sun had set. The stars of freedom shone once more.

TANKS ROLLED INTO SANTO TOMAS, AND U.S. troops poured in behind them.

"Oh God, I was happy!" said Sally Blaine. She discovered that the young soldier who'd driven the first tank was from her home county in Missouri.

Then stretchers arrived, carrying the men wounded in the fight to get there. Frankie's combat-nursing experience flooded back as she and the other nurses rushed with renewed energy to care for the wounded soldiers. The women settled seventeen injured men in a first-floor dormitory room turned clinic.

Frankie volunteered in the surgery, where, shortly, medics carried in two badly injured and unconscious American soldiers. One man's foot had been shattered. A priest held a Coleman lantern over the operating table as Frankie assisted a surgeon in amputating the foot.

Lying in the hospital, Rita Palmer heard an American GI swearing. She jumped from her bed and helped tend the wounded, wearing shorts and a pajama top.

The nurses worked through the night, side by side with the Army doctors and medics who had come through the gates with the liberators. Several nurses fainted from fatigue during the long, strenuous hours, but their experience on Bataan and Corregidor helped them cope. They also discovered that the practice of medicine had advanced without them. A doctor asked Rita to fetch some "penicillin," and she hadn't a clue what he meant.

Later Frankie checked on the soldier who'd lost his foot. As she watched the unconscious man rest, her compassion welled up, and she

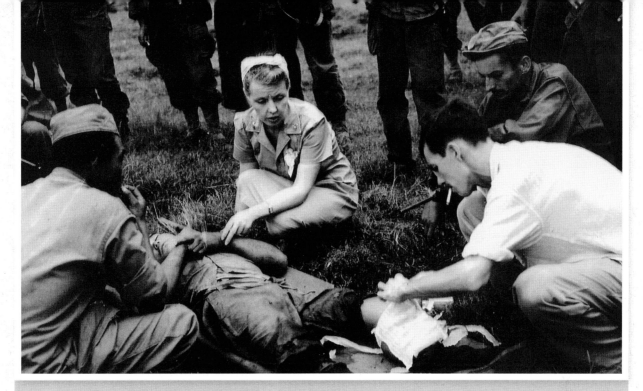

Army Nurse Frankie Lewey treats a wounded man shortly after liberation.

burst into tears. At that moment First Lieutenant Francis Jerrett opened his eyes and smiled. Frankie's breath caught. She knew she had endured the years of imprisonment with her heart intact.

First Lieutenant Jerrett had been wounded in the fierce street battle to push back the Japanese so that U.S. forces could get to Santo Tomas. He wrote home later that he had opened his eyes in the hospital to see a beautiful angel crying for him. A man known to run from any woman who batted her eyes at him, Jerrett said, "It was love at first sight."

Morning dawned, the first in three years the nurses did not have to line up for roll call. More U.S. troops rode in on a strange new vehicle called a jeep. They dug foxholes and set up machine guns and artillery.

And they carried food. The men shared their rations and handed out chocolate. The soldiers themselves proved good medicine for the nurses. Next to the emaciated prison survivors, the men stood tall and hearty, their skin pink with health, their eyes alive.

"We had good army chow today! No food had ever tasted this good! No food had ever made people more ill!" said American internee Tressa Cates, a civilian nurse who worked in the camp hospital with the Army nurses. Their bodies too starved to digest food, "a few hours later hundreds of us were seized with cramps and diarrhea, and many of us were too ill and weak to reach the toilets."

That first day of freedom went too fast for Denny Williams. "It was too confusing, too distracting for us to take in all that was happening," she said. "We went about much as we had all the days before, still intimidated, still keeping face, still following our captivity routines."

Told by the sergeant in charge that they could send messages home to their families, Army Nurse Sallie Durrett asked, "How many words can we put on this message?"

"Hell, lady, you're an American. Put as many words as you want to," he said.

Outside the walls and in the sky above, the battle for Manila continued to rage.

"As the shells tore through the air above us, we ducked each time, as though that would have saved us. We remained unconcerned. We thought only of eating, and the presence of our soldiers made us feel immune to danger," said Tressa Cates.

On February 7, the Japanese began heavy shelling of the Santo Tomas neighborhood. Army Nurse Beatrice Chambers stood in line to use the toilets until she realized they weren't flushing and walked away. Seconds later a bomb smashed through the wall and killed the people in line where she had stood. Fifteen internees who had struggled and survived three years of captivity lost their lives the first morning of that attack.

"We were stunned and almost in a state of shock as we went about our work cleaning up the rubble and caring for the wounded and dying," said Tressa Cates. "Stunned and weeping relatives walked through the narrow aisles to identify their dead and wounded, while doctors and nurses tried to do their work."

Before the battle ended, thirty-two internees died, and two hundred suffered wounds. Nurses mourned the death of a doctor they had worked with throughout their captivity.

The same day U.S. forces freed Santo To-mas, they liberated Bilibid Prison, where some of the men captured on Bataan and Corregidor were POWs. In a secret raid four days earlier, Americans had freed five hundred other POW men from Cabanatuan prison camp. The men, starving and severely ill, were brought to the Santo Tomas hospital. A number of women from Santo Tomas joyfully reunited with their husbands, who had survived the Bataan Death March and imprisonment. Others learned their husbands would never return. Many had been shipped to forced-labor camps in Japan. Rita Palmer and Denny Williams received no news about their husbands.

Internees take cover during shelling, as the battle for Manila continues outside Santo Tomas gates.

U.S. Army nurses arrive to relieve POW nurses. First Lieutenant Rita Palmer hugs an old friend, Second Lieutenant Dorothy Davis.

SIX DAYS AFTER LIBERATION, ONE HUNDRED Army nurses from the States flew into Manila to take over from the POW nurses at Santo Tomas. Like the soldiers, the new arrivals bloomed with vigor and health. Sally Blaine said that next to them she felt like an old woman. But finally the nurses from Bataan and Corregidor could safely rest.

Sally learned from the relief nurses that the Army Nurse Corps now had military rank. Sally was no longer Miss Blaine but Lieutenant Blaine. Another surprise—Army nurses could get married without needing to resign. Four nurses tied the knot that week.

Still, the freedom for which the POW nurses had yearned suddenly opened a world of uncertainty. Their joy and relief mingled with worries about how they would reenter a life of freedom they could barely remember.

An Army major recognized Sally and asked, "Aren't you one of our girls?"

"Yes, I am."

"Would you like to go home?"

The enduring composure Sally had mustered in the Bataan jungle and preserved through captivity crumbled. At last, she could allow herself to believe she'd see her home and family again. Finally it was safe to cry, and Sally wept.

The next day Army nurses discovered they would be the first internees to leave Santo Tomas and evacuate the Philippines. The sixty-eight women climbed into trucks one more time on the morning of February 14. A huge crowd gathered in front of the main building to send them off. Nurses waved good-bye and exited the iron gates of Santo Tomas onto España Boulevard, headed for a makeshift airstrip and their flight to freedom.

Los Baños Internment Camp

AS THE NURSES IN SANTO TOMAS CELEBRATED their freedom, Navy nurses in Los Baños wondered if American forces even knew their camp existed. Months earlier, when U.S. planes flew over in September 1944, nurses believed they'd soon be free. Through October, November, and December they saw more planes. An orange tinge of fire or the black smoke of bombings would sometimes appear at the edge of the sky. But they remained prisoners.

On Christmas Eve, Peggy Nash went to midnight Mass in the barracks chapel. Nativity figures crafted from sand, as well as the simple, candlelit altar, looked beautiful as Peggy knelt to pray. The next morning, hundreds of American planes roared over the camp. Prisoners cheered. Christmas had come, and freedom was so close, Peggy could taste it.

Yet in the days and weeks to follow, the liberators did not come. Fear clung to Peggy like a shadow. Drugs and medical supplies ran out. There was no adhesive to apply dressings. The death rate climbed. Little wood remained to build coffins, and few men had strength enough to dig graves or carry the dead to the cemetery. "We realized that it was no longer a question of our liberators coming, but our survival until they arrived," said Navy Nurse Edwina Todd.

News of liberation at Santo Tomas had leaked into Los Baños in early February. Three weeks later Japanese troops still controlled the Laguna de Bay region.

Two hundred Imperial soldiers stood guard at Los Baños, and they had ringed the camp with machine guns pointed inward at the prisoners. A rumor swept the camp, and the captives, who hadn't eaten in two days, believed it. The Japanese army planned to execute them.

The morning of February 23, Peggy heard a plane fly over, and she stepped outside to take a look. It was shortly before roll call, and the Japanese soldiers gathered in the field across the road from the hospital for their daily calisthenics. Peggy noticed leaflets falling from the plane, and moments later more planes appeared, and more white scraps floated down. The realization came suddenly. Not leaflets—parachutes.

Peggy gazed in amazement at the men dropping from the sky and landing a short distance beyond the camp's barbed-wire fence. She had never seen or heard of paratroopers. The men from the 11th Airborne Division hit the ground, came up with machine guns stuttering, and took out the perimeter guards.

"Dear God," Peggy said, "today we either live or die, but at least this suffering is going to be over. And then I said a Hail Mary and an Act of Contrition that the sisters always told us to say."

The crack of gunfire and grenade explosions sounded near the front gate. Filipino guerrillas and U.S. Army Rangers charged in. Everything happened at once. Bullets flew in all directions. Down went the camp fence, and in barreled humongous boxy vehicles on tractor-treads. U.S. intelligence had turned up evidence that the Japanese soldiers at Los

Baños had orders to kill all the prisoners after they finished their exercise regimen that morning.

Peggy ran up to one of the paratroopers. "Do you have any food?" she cried. "You've gotta get out of here," he told her, pulling out a Hershey bar.

Peggy stuffed it into her pocket and ran into the hospital. She plucked up the baby, Elizabeth, whom she had delivered five days ago. Soldiers carried her, the baby, and the baby's mother on stretchers to one of the strange vehicles.

"Run, run, run to the beach!" yelled American soldiers. But many prisoners were too weak to move. Others wanted to pack their belongings. Troops set the barracks ablaze to hurry people along. Americans had killed all the Japanese in Los Baños, but close to a thousand enemy soldiers, very much alive, were camped only eight miles away. If they discovered the escaping prisoners, it was unlikely the small group of American liberators would be able to stop the Japanese from killing them all.

Internees unable to walk the mile and a half to Laguna de Bay were loaded into the amphibious tanks, which Peggy learned were called amtracs.

"We were lucky we got to ride," Peggy said, watching Los Baños going up in flames behind them. Her friend Navy Nurse Susie Pitcher and others followed on foot. "I saw all those poor girls dragging . . . swollen with beriberi."

All 2,100 captives headed for the beach. To reach safety behind American lines, they would have to escape under the noses of the Japanese, then across the waters of Laguna de Bay.

U.S. Army paratroopers landing outside Los Baños Internment Camp, part of a multipronged assault including Filipino guerrillas and a recon platoon, which crossed Laguna de Bay two nights before. February 23, 1945.

Once at the beach, Peggy got off the amtrac to sit down, rest, and wait for those on foot. Suddenly Japanese snipers opened fire. "I covered the baby with a great big hat, and I lay down on the sand over her. Later, I took the baby and started running across the beach, found an amtrac, got on it, and somebody said we'd better shove off, because the Japanese were reloading."

Peggy, baby, and mother arrived at the village of Mamatid, in American-controlled territory, an hour later. They journeyed by truck and ambulance to a relief center in Manila, where everyone was fed. All eleven Navy nurses had survived. Now, once again, they used their nursing skills to aid others.

CHAPTER 18
HOMECOMING

The Army nurses flew to Leyte, a Philippine island solidly in U.S. control. Arriving at the 126th Army General Hospital, the women were amazed by advances made in army medicine and facilities during the war. Mostly they appreciated the simple things: bathing and toilet facilities, real mattresses, pillows, and clean sheets. The opportunity to rest—without fear—was priceless.

Seventeen of the nurses were so sick they were immediately admitted to the hospital and given intravenous fluids. Starvation and a bowel obstruction had taken the "stiff" from the starch of sixty-year-old Maude Davison. Sally Blaine shivered with malarial chills and fever. Ethel Thor suffered a painful suppurating ulcer where her back had rubbed against the truck on the ride from Santo Tomas. Frances Nash hobbled on legs swollen from beriberi.

Doctors gave the women complete physicals and lab tests. Army nurses at the hospital offered their own bras and underwear to the women, plus lipsticks, lotions, and nail polish. The Army outfitted them with brand-new olive-green uniforms flown in from Australia.

Forty-nine of the women were healthy enough to leave the medical ward and move to a convalescent hospital on a secluded Leyte beach. Rita Palmer headed for the waves in a borrowed swimsuit, starkly aware of how emaciated she looked.

The women learned to eat with a knife and fork again. They ate five-course meals served on white linen, though it sometimes made them sick because starvation had ravaged their digestive systems. They feasted on cookies and ice cream, drank soda, and watched American movies.

Reporters came to interview them, writing about the nurses' valor and their "wonderful" American womanhood. Attorneys listened to details of the horrors they had experienced and witnessed, taking notes for war-crimes trials.

A week later the group, minus eleven not yet well enough to travel, flew to Hawaii and set foot on home soil at last. Landing at Hickam Field, several nurses knelt and kissed the ground. Nurses took their first paycheck in over three years to the Post Exchange, buying new shoes, lipstick, perfume, and purses.

The following day the Army nurses flew from Hawaii to San Francisco. Fifteen thousand people gathered to greet them at Hamilton Field. As the women disembarked, family and friends who had managed to get there rushed forward to grab them, touch them, kiss and hug them. They were welcomed home in a highly orchestrated ceremony of speeches,

Opposite: Liberated Army nurses take off for home in a C-54 transport plane.

Above: Army nurses being awarded promotions, battle ribbons, and Bronze Stars for valor by Brigadier General Guy B. Denit. February 20, 1945.

band music, and one blinding flashbulb after another.

The nurses believed they had simply done their job and didn't like all the fuss. They were relieved to be driven to Letterman Army Hospital, where they enjoyed privacy, phone calls to family, and more rest.

Three days later, the nurses endured further ceremony. The Purple Heart was awarded to nurses Rita Palmer and Rosemary Hogan for their injuries in the bombing of Hospital No. 1. In a cross-country phone call, Rita assured her mother she was fine. "I gained twenty pounds in twenty days," she said.

The next week some of the survivors of the Bataan Death March also came to Letterman.

"Smitty!" cried Frankie Lewey to a former patient. "Let me look at you! Fine angel I was, leaving you there on Bataan in a body cast!" Nurses were heavy-hearted that so many men had perished but amazed by those who had survived.

Alice Zwicker marveled at several amputees. "They made their own peg legs," she said.

When the women were healthy enough, they left Letterman for sixty days' leave to visit family. Waiting for the plane that would take her to El Paso, Hattie Brantley felt sorely alone. "I'd had someone right beside me every minute for years," she said. "All of a sudden I was sitting beside people who didn't know me—people I didn't know." Hattie planned to kiss the Texas soil, but she didn't have to. Stepping off the plane, the blowing Texas sand slapped her in the face.

The women soon saw that America had changed during the war years. Everything moved faster, from the pace people walked, to the cars driving by on the streets. The nurses noticed small changes, too, such as the fact that nearly all women now wore earrings.

"It all seemed like the movies," Madeline Ullom said. "People moving about dressed in pretty clothes. They weren't acting. They were living."

Despite war rationing of food and gasoline, Americans lived in luxury compared to prison-camp life. The nurses felt alien and isolated. Some faced fresh grief.

Sally Blaine learned her mother was dying and rushed back to Missouri just in time to say good-bye. Another nurse's mother had died a mere three days before Santo Tomas was liberated.

News trickled in about the male POWs from Bataan and Corregidor. Rita Palmer and Denny Williams learned their husbands had not survived.

Dorothy Scholl was one of the lucky few nurses whose sweetheart had lived, not only through the Bataan Death March but also a prison-ship voyage and POW camp in Japan. For three and a half years she had feared that her fiancé, Harold Armold, was dead. At Letterman word came—he was alive. When Harold returned to the States in the fall, he contacted Dorothy, and the two were reunited at Fitzsimmons Army General Hospital in Colorado and married soon after.

Frances Nash returned to her family's farm in Georgia.

"This is the greatest day of our lives," her father said.

"I'm numb, really, just numb," Frances said. The bounty of food astounded her. "At dinner the other night we had steak, more steak than I could eat, and I carefully cut off half the meat and asked my mother to put it away for the following day. . . . Mother was hurt because I didn't think there was any more in the kitchen. When you've eaten boiled canna bulbs, you have a tendency to think about the next meal."

While other nurses traveled home, Ethel Thor stayed at Letterman, receiving skin grafts to heal the sore on her back. Ethel, Frankie Lewey, and several other nurses remained emotionally unsettled for some time. When she was able, Ethel took a twenty-nine-day leave, riding the train home to Tacoma, Washington, where she was reunited with her sister Vivian and nieces.

When Ethel returned to active duty stateside in July 1945, she suffered nervousness and bouts of crying, making it difficult to do her tasks. Though diagnosed with severe and chronic anxiety, Ethel remained on duty until the Army retired her that September.

Frankie remained hospitalized through the end of March, when she went home to Oklahoma. Her sixty-day leave was extended to ninety days, after which she went to an Army redistribution center in Miami Beach, Florida, for further convalescence. The Army had established a number of centers around the country where American POWs from Europe, as well as the Pacific, went to rest and regain their health.

Sally Blaine met "Zip" Millett at one of the centers. An Army colonel, Zip had fought in Europe and been taken prisoner by the Ger-

FINAL EXTRA

THE DENVER POST

WEDNESDAY, NOVEMBER 7, 1945

Love in Manila

during the days of the defense of Bataan and Corregidor resulted in the marriage in Evergreen, Colo., last week of Capt. Harold A. Armold and First Lieut. Dorothy Scholl. They met again in Fitzsimons General hospital recently after three years of Japanese imprisonment, during which each feared the other dead, and renewed their marriage plans.

EX-WAR PRISONERS WED IN EVERGREEN

Engagement Which Began in Philippines Ends in Marriage for Capt. Harold A. Armold and First Lieut. Dorothy Scholl.

An engagement, which began in Manila shortly before the defense of Bataan and Corregidor, ended in marriage in the Episcopal church in Evergreen last Thursday for Capt. Harold A. Armold and First Lieut. Dorothy Scholl, after four years of waiting, worry and fear. On the night Captain Armold was taken prisoner at Bataan, Lieutenant Scholl, an army nurse, was evacuated to Corregidor. Neither knew what became of the other and thru three and a half years of imprisonment each feared the other was dead. When they met again recently at Fitzsimons General hospital, where both were convalescing, their marriage planning was resumed.

"We are just two inconspicuous people who got married," they commented reticently when asked about their romantic story.

Opposite: Major Juanita Redmond pins a Purple Heart on First Lieutenant Rosemary Hogan. Both women were on duty at Bataan Hospital No. 1 when it was bombed and Rosemary wounded.

Above: This news clipping tells the romantic story of First Lieutenant Dorothy Scholl's wedding.

mans. Sally and Zip hit it off immediately and soon married. "I was sure there weren't going to be any more horrible things in our lives," said Sally.

After visiting home in New Hampshire, Rita Palmer went on a recruiting drive for the Army Nurse Corps. She spent eighteen days in New York City. "We had a ball going to plays and painting our fingernails, going to Elizabeth Arden and getting all gussied up."

Other nurses resented being forced to put up a front for the public. "The Army sent us around all over the place making speeches for the war bonds. It was terrible, because you didn't want to do it," Millie Dalton said. "You were so tired, you just wanted to rest and be with your family."

"You had to sort of catch up on what life was all about," Charlie Dworsky said. "You were suddenly thrown into chaos and confusion. Everybody wanted to talk to you. Everybody wanted you to make a speech. And you were suffering from malnutrition; you were a nervous wreck."

Navy Nurse Dorothy Still said, "I began to feel like an object after a while, sort of a freak."

MID-MARCH 1945
Wilkes-Barre, Pennsylvania

THE LIBERATED NAVY NURSES ARRIVED AT OAK Knoll Naval Hospital in California with little fanfare in mid-March. One nurse's knees kept buckling from beriberi; another's heart was so weakened, she could hardly walk; and a third had difficulty breathing.

While she was in captivity, Peggy Nash's weight had dropped from 130 to 68 pounds and doctors said she was too sick to go home.

"They took X-ray after X-ray and kept telling me I had a cavity in my chest. Then they told me they'd better take me closer to home, because I had tuberculosis and only five years to live." Doctors transferred her to a TB sanitarium in Long Island, New York.

Peggy Nash's mother had seen the photo of her daughter in prison camp in 1942. Afterward, she'd heard no news of Peggy for three anxious years. Mrs. Nash had sickened of people calling to ask about her daughter and had her phone disconnected. In her fear of getting word that Peggy was dead, Mrs. Nash refused

-J Day: County's only female POW looks back

EDITOR'S NOTE: It was years ago today that the anese surrendered. For former area woman the has special meaning.

OM MOONEY
Writer

Margaret Nash thought the world was coming to an end. It was early uary 1943. She and her fel-Navy nurses were trapped anila, capital of the Phil-nes. They were watching Invading Japanese lower American flag and run up r own rising sun banner.

Editorial — Page 2B.

he nurses had no idea what ld become of themselves or r hundreds of patients, tly military men hurt in ceaseless bombing of the eding weeks. ut they knew for certain were prisoners of war. We just cried," said Miss ... "It was just terrible." or Miss Nash, then 31, it a long way from the family e at 8 Oxford St. in Hano-Township and from her her, brothers and sisters. he 11 Navy nurses in Ma-the three civilian nurses accompanied them and 66 y nurses, also in the Phil-nes, would be the only rican nurses to spend the in a prison camp. here was something else

unique about Miss Nash. Of the 329 people from Luzerne Coun-ty listed as captured or missing in action during World War II, she was the only woman. Miss Nash was born in Edwardsville. Her family even-tually moved to Hanover Town-

ship, where she graduated from high school in June 1929. The next month she entered the Wilkes-Barre Mercy Hospi-tal School of Nursing, graduat-ing in 1932. At first she worked as a pri-vate duty nurse. Then for 18

months she worked in a tuber-culosis sanitarium in New York state. "But my mother decided I better come home because she was concerned I might get TB (tuberculosis)," said Miss Nash. Her uncle, Congressman C,

Murray Turpin, recommended she give the United States Na-vy Nurse Corps a try, and she took his advice. By October 1940, she was stationed on the Pacific Island of Guam. She thoroughly en-joyed her work as an operating room supervisor and a teacher of hospital work to corpsmen and orderlies. In September 1941, when Miss Nash and a group of other nurses were transferred to the Philippines, they were dressed in black and carried in ships painted black. The war was getting closer. There she was assigned to the Canacao Hospital, near the Cavite Navy Yard, south of the capital city of Manila. Still, she said, "I never thought we were going to have war. We continued on with our work and our social life." Then, early on a morning in December, the telephone in the nurses' quarters rang. The Jap-anese had bombed Pearl Har-bor, in Hawaii; the United States was at war. Knowing attack by the Japa-nese was imminent, the Navy nurse crew, headed by Lt. Commander Laura Cobb, helped send as many patients as possible out of the country. A few days later the Japa-nese bombed Cavite, and the nurses got their first real taste of war. "I think it started to sink in at that time," Miss Nash said. "It was a massacre. It seemed there was fire all around us, all around the hospital. I kept thinking, 'how could anyone do this?'"

(Continued on Page 7A)

Thousands of people welcomed Margaret Nash, center, upon her return to Wilkes-Barre

---

to answer the door or allow anyone but family into her house.

John McSweeney, editor of the local news-paper, was a neighbor. He discovered through news channels that Peggy was alive and free. McSweeney notified Peggy's brother James, a Hanover Township policeman, and James went to his mother's home to deliver the good news.

Two weeks later, when her mother fell sick, doctors allowed Peggy Nash to leave the hospital for ten days. As her train pulled into Wilkes-Barre, Peggy saw hundreds of people filling the rail yard.

"What are all those people out there for?" she wondered.

She stepped off the train, and the crowd started cheering. "God bless you! Welcome home! Hiya, Margaret!"

The local high school band played music, and huge banners welcomed Peggy. The mayor gave her keys to the city. An estimated twenty-five thousand people stood waiting for the hometown heroine to go by in an open car. Schoolchildren had been given the day off to see the "remarkable lady" returning from three years as a POW. Some said it was one of the biggest parades ever in Wilkes-Barre.

People ran up and gave Peggy flowers as the car drove slowly along the familiar streets hung with American flags. The motorcade stopped at St. Aloysius Church, and the parish Boy Scouts ushered her inside. Peggy knelt before the altar to give thanks. As she left the church, tears streamed down her cheeks.

"This is what I was waiting for," she said.

Driving up Oxford Street, Peggy stood in the moving car, eager for a glimpse of home. Seeing her mother on the porch, she stretched out her arms. Awash in tears, she called out, "Mother! Mother!"

Moments later, Peggy was in her mother's arms, home at last.

1945
United States of America

Army and Navy POW nurses returning from the Philippines had one simple desire—to get on with their lives. "They shared an incredible amount between them . . . formed a really strong bond," says Sandy Thor, Ethel's youngest daughter. "That gave them strength and helped them survive." But now they went their separate ways, disbanding their wartime surrogate family.

"The trouble started almost immediately; I just didn't know it at the time. We all put on a lot of weight right away. . . . I was having dry skin and depression and a lot of things like that," Millie Dalton said.

"I got home in March, met my husband on May 11, married him on July 11. I didn't keep in touch with the other nurses. I went to the doctor, and I told him all my troubles. And he said, 'Well, sweetie, there's nothing wrong with your appetite, is there?' I never went back to him."

For the most part, the women dealt by themselves with whatever troubles arose. They

By Bamboo Telegraph:
GI Life And Death In The Pacific
Atrocity Story: Japs Steal Nurse's Black Nightgown

That our Japanese enemies will stoop to anything is evidenced by what happened to the black nightgown of Army Nurse Rita G. Palmer.

During the entire time she spent in a Jap prison camp after the fall of Corregidor, this indignant young lady planned to relate the pillaging of her nightgown to the War Crimes Commission investigating war atrocities.

One reason the swiping of the nightgown was such a cruel blow

to Nurse Palmer was that the filmy garment had enabled her to feel well-dressed as she dashed into bomb shelters during night attacks on Corregidor.

Once she bumped into a general, who took one look at her and two looks at her nightgown, and gasped: "Where do you think you're going in that!"

Then the Japs came and removed her from Corregidor to a prison camp on the Philippine mainland. During her removal, her nightgown disappeared.

Now safe in the states, she has a new black nightgown, with lace and everything—an exact replica of the one she lost on Corregidor. It was given to her as a birthday present—by other nurses who had listened to the story of how she became nightgownless and endured three years of Jap imprisonment.

Sister Nurses Replace Rita's Black Nightie

HONOLULU, Feb. 24.— (UP) — (delayed) — Lt. Rita Palmer of Hampton, N. H., one of the 68 Bataan nurses enroute by air to the states, had a brand new nightgown today — a "daring job" in black lace.

Her siste[r] for her [...] shopping t[...]

Rita, a t[...] was one [...] wounded c[...] other was [...] gan of Cha[...]

What m[...] special wa[...] For even [...] terror of [...] to her bl[...] when ther[...] ties for sle[...] ing it whe[...]

Claudette [...] enacted th[...] picture, "[...] Hail."

Today th[...] the nurses [...] gift shop [...] ment" for [...] nocently oc[...] with the pu[...] suit.

The or[...] was torn [...] wounds.

Left: Untrue stories about POW nurses circulated by word-of-mouth and newsprint (left). The story in the image below was written by Army Nurse Rosemary Hogan to debunk such rumors. For the most part, the nurses had to focus on getting well and rebuilding their lives, and they couldn't spare the energy to fight salacious stories told about them.

Liberty
THE MAGAZINE OF A FREE PEOPLE

Three long years after their capture at Corregidor, the Angels of Bataan were glad to leave Santo Tomas—even in a truck.

What Did *Not* Happen to the Bataan Nurses

BY CAPTAIN ROSEMARY HOGAN
ARMY NURSE CORPS, A.A.F.

Capt. Rosemary Hogan, A.N.C.

A nurse who fell captive to the Japs on Corregidor tells about the treatment accorded this brave band of American women. It's not what you've heard before — but it's the

AS the home folks back in Chattanooga, Oklahoma, got the story, the Japs had chopped off my arms, cut out my tongue, and left me pregnant. Just to vary the theme, someone said my legs had been amputated.

All this was going on when I was still in Santo Tomas helping take care of troops wounded in liberating us from the Jap internment camp.

After all the terrible, and terribly true, stories about Jap atrocities against soldiers and civilians, I suppose it was just too much for the people in the States to believe that any of us — the sixty-eight nurses from Bataan — could have escaped the same beastly treatment.

Take the infantryman who had been celebrating the capture of Santo Tomas on beer.

This soldier strolled casually into our little hospital, stopped, and stared in amazement to find Army

"Well, tell me," he said, "how did the Japs treat you?"

"It could have been worse," I said.

"Didn't they do anything to you?"

"Sure. They locked us up in this place."

"Damn it," he insisted, "I mean, did they rape you?"

Even the wounded, as they came in on their litters, wanted to know. Were we really the nurses from Bataan? They couldn't believe that we could have arms and legs, much less be alive, after nearly three years of captivity.

I never heard the ghastly rumors about myself until I had been home a week. Then a girl friend said:

"I guess you've heard all the frightful things that have been said about you?"

I had not, but it seemed that an officer from Fort Sill, Oklahoma, where I had been stationed before the war, called this girl and asked her, "Did you hear what happened did not have counseling or antidepressant medication available as we do today. The few who wanted to talk frankly about their experience in combat and captivity got a rude awakening.

Navy Nurse Dorothy Still's attempt at being honest went something like this:

"My dear lieutenant! I love your display of ribbons! I'm dying to hear what it was like!"

"It was rough at times, but . . ."

"Oh, yes, I know exactly what you mean. . . . It's been rough here, let me tell you. We've had to stand in line for hours to get meat stamps and gasoline stamps. Have you tried to find nylons? They're simply not to be had."

People kept telling Army Nurse Eleanor Garen to just forget. She tried. "But I wasn't able to, and when I tried to talk about it, a few people said, 'Oh, you're bragging'—stuff like that. I said, 'No, I'm not bragging, I was there. That's three years out of my life. Why can't I talk about it?' Even other nurses weren't willing to listen. Nobody was."

Many people assumed the nurses had been raped by their captors. Army Nurse Rosemary Hogan wrote a magazine article entitled "What Did *Not* Happen to the Bataan Nurses" to dispel rumors that the Japanese had "chopped off my arms, cut out my tongue, and left me pregnant."

One of the first questions to greet Hattie Brantley in her hometown was "Well, where's your baby?"

Even her mother was scandalized to hear that the camp guards had peered in at the women showering. "What in the world did you do?" she asked.

"I put my wash rag over my face," Hattie said.

After four grim years of war, Americans wanted heroines to raise their spirits. But no framework existed in the 1940s for people to understand women who had acted with enduring courage and strength on the battlefield and as prisoners of war—women who had acted like men.

Combat veterans were men. No woman had earned the Combat Infantry Badge, and history would focus on those who had earned this distinction. The former POW nurses were told by their superiors to sign statements agreeing not to speak publicly of the atrocities they had seen.

At Hattie's Army reorientation in Little Rock, Arkansas, she was told, "'Now you're going off to your assignments, and whatever you do, just keep it to yourself, don't talk about it.' They absolutely told us that. They treated it as if it was a stigma."

Newspaper reporters, civic leaders, and neighbors cast the returning nurses into categories people were familiar with, either exaggerating their femininity or imagining salacious behavior. Postwar doctors and psychologists treating POWs focused on the men.

Today's diagnosis of post-traumatic stress disorder (PTSD) confirms that people can suffer severe anxiety for years after exposure to traumatic events and that they need treatment—psychotherapy, medications, or both. When the POW nurses came home, public understanding of PTSD was two wars and generations away. Even family members and close friends could not understand what these women had gone through and how it now shaped them. The nurses missed one another, and they had nothing like Facebook or texting to keep in touch.

Nurses who had escaped Corregidor before the surrender had troubles, too, when they arrived home in 1942. Lucy Wilson weighed only seventy pounds and suffered blackouts, one time while driving a car. Once, she broke into tears at the beauty parlor, unable to stop thinking about the terrible things she had witnessed.

Lucy received hundreds of letters from people asking if she knew this or that soldier who had fought on Bataan or Corregidor. "The mother of a young man I knew talked to me, and I'll never forget the emotional and mental torture it was for me to tell her that her son was dead," Lucy said. "I guess that was about the nearest I ever came to a breakdown."

Many of the nurses faced continued illness. Two Army nurses remained hospitalized for many months with severe hepatitis. Another continued a decade-long battle with amoebic dysentery, while doctors dismissed one woman's TB complaints until she became so sick, she had to be hospitalized for a year and a half. Alice Zwicker spent seven years in a TB hospital. Many of the nurses suffered permanent damage to their intestinal tracts. Most had stopped menstruating during captivity. Peggy Nash's menstrual cycle never resumed. Rita Palmer suffered a number of miscarriages. Depression was common.

One year after liberation, Eleanor Garen wrote, "I have often wondered why I survived. . . . What purpose have I in life? It is ashes in my mouth, so futile, so useless to myself as well as to others."

"I came back, and I was losing my mind," admitted Peggy Nash. "I was young, and I thought my life was over." Peggy had been planning her wedding when the war started. Months after returning to the U.S., she heard the first news of Ed in five years.

"His ship had a direct hit, and most of his men were killed," said Peggy. But her fiancé managed to swim ashore, where he was captured and sent to Japan. Ed survived four years as a POW.

"After he was back, I sort of got him over the shock. At least we were alive. Then I canceled the wedding because I had TB and doctors said I would never have any children." Peggy never told Ed that doctors had given her only five years to live.

The Navy retired Peggy for medical reasons in 1946 but gave her the honorary rank of lieutenant commander. She remained in treatment at St. Alban's Naval Hospital in New York for tuberculosis and tropical diseases, including beriberi.

"I was determined not to die," Peggy said. Eventually, her health improved enough for her to leave the sanitarium, but she wasn't cured of TB. "Every time I'd get a job, it would start again. I thought—is this going to be my life? I thought I'd lose my mind and end up in a mental institution."

Peggy's friend Susie Pitcher was so ill with beriberi that Navy doctors gave her the same life expectancy as Peggy. Their prediction proved true when Susie died five years later.

Peggy's doctor suggested she go west, where the climate might improve her health. In California, she got a part-time desk job at the Student Health Center at University of California, Berkeley. This enabled her to catch up on advances in medicine while gaining emotional stability.

The Army sent Frankie Lewey back to active duty in November 1945. By December 12, arthritis forced her back into the hospital. Her sick leave was extended several more months before the Army declared her fit for limited duty. She wanted to leave the Army and applied for disability retirement.

Frankie's doctor testified to the Army Retirement Board in June 1946 that Frankie was permanently disabled. A board member asked Frankie which of her joints was bothered by arthritis.

"Well, sir, I can't truthfully tell you any joint that does not hurt," Frankie testified. "It hurts me from my neck on down and up my spine, particularly there in my shoulder joints. . . . At times, my feet and ankles are so swollen that it is difficult to get about."

Her doctor also testified that Frankie's state of mind made her unfit for duty, citing her "nervousness, tremors of the hands and voice, hyper-excitability, and hostility toward the examiner . . . stress, severe, this patient having undergone three years as a POW suffering a multitude of illnesses."

Despite the doctor's and her own testimony, the board sent Frankie back to active duty.

The Army did retire Josie Nesbit with 100 percent disability at the end of 1945, just shy of her fifty-second birthday.

Commander Maude Davidson wanted to return to active duty, but since she was sixty and in poor health, the Army retired her in January 1946. The Army had been her entire life for nearly thirty years. She considered it her family.

"They'll take care of me when I need them," she said, but she did not register for Veterans Administration benefits.

Maude had pulled her nurses together as a unit, insisting on discipline, order, and dedication to their patients. This "prescription for endurance and courage" had kept her nurses alive.

Army doctors who served with Maude nominated her for a Distinguished Service Medal for valor and sacrifice on Bataan and Corregidor, but Army brass decided Maude deserved merely a commendation for a job well done.

Chief Nurse Ann Mealor was praised publicly by General Jonathan Wainwright for her refusal to leave the island before it fell to the Japanese. He called her decision "one of the most courageous acts of the entire campaign: . . . I consider—and still consider—this a truly great act of heroism. She knew as well as I that she was signing her captivity warrant." Still, Ann never received a medal or commendation for her brave and loyal action.

Dr. Dana Nance, the civilian medical director at the Los Baños prison camp, wrote to the Navy High Command recommending a special

Former Army nurse POWs after their arrival in the continental United States with the Chief of the Army Nurse Corps, Colonel Mary B. Phillips. Hamilton Field, California, February 24, 1945. Left to right: First Lieutenant Verna Henson, Colonel Phillips, and First Lieutenant Madeline Ullom.

unit commendation for Peggy Nash, her Chief Nurse Laura Mae Cobb, and the nine Navy nurse POWs.

"They gave unstintingly of their time and professional skill beyond the call of duty for the alleviation of suffering of the fellow civilian internees," he said. His effort failed, and the case faded away.

Promoted to major, Maude Davison retired to California, where she married a friend from before her Army days. When she suffered a massive stroke that left her in a coma, the local Veterans Administration (VA) hospital refused to care for her. Her husband had to petition the regional VA office to get her a bed. She died on June 11, 1956.

Though many of the nurses received short shrift from the VA, they were not the kind of women to complain. Forty years passed before they began to speak out and gain recognition

for their sacrifices. Madeline Ullom testified before the U.S. Senate Veterans Affairs Committee on January 26, 1982. "No one ever gave this group of women the recognition they earned and deserved." Madeline further testified:

When separated from the Army, I did not request a disability. Not until later did I apply to the VA for compensation, and I was granted 30% disability for arthritis I contracted during my stay in prison camp. I have a great reluctance now to apply for further disability because I am acutely aware that such application results only in a hassle. . . . The stories I hear concerning applications for further disability have long ago discouraged me. Further, I know dozens of my nurse companions who have made application and have met with nothing but opposition.

Madeline questioned the VA spending thousands of dollars on a study that concluded that the nurses' POW experience was unequaled in the annals of American history and yet denied these women just compensation.

I cannot fathom how the VA cannot make good on its promises. Of our original 68 nurses, twenty-six have died since our release. I do not, and I repeat, I DO NOT BELIEVE ALL OF THEIR DEATHS WERE ATTRIBUTABLE TO OLD AGE, although some Veterans Administration individuals would have us believe so. I am convinced their death was premature and directly related to their stay in a Japanese prison camp.

Ethel Thor asked for nothing from her government until nearly ten years after the war, when she heard she might be entitled to compensation through the War Claims Commission. Her application received this reply:

Your claim for compensation for inhumane treatment . . . was adjudicated, and an award in the sum of $1,505.00 has been made to you. However, the Commission cannot certify your claim to the Treasury for payment at this time, since the money in the War Claims Fund for payment of such claims was exhausted as of the close of business May 22, 1953.

The money had run out thirty-one days before Ethel made her claim.

Army Nurse Sallie Durrett's intestinal system never returned to normal. "In 1978 the problem seemed to be becoming more severe, and I went to the VA and asked for an evaluation."

The Veterans Administration ruled that Sallie suffered no disability. She received no benefits until Congress passed the Former Prisoners of War Benefit Act in 1981. This law mandated medical and dental care for POWs. At that time Sallie was reevaluated and assigned 30 percent disability.

Millie Dalton's POW years continued to plague her. "I had beriberi, which damaged my nerves, and I still have peripheral neuropathy from that. . . . I had problems with my stomach, still do."

Perhaps the worst consequence was Millie's anxiety seventy years later. "I still dream about the Japanese coming after me," she said. "If somebody comes in the room and I don't know they're there and they tap me on the shoulder, I'll jump out of my skin."

CHAPTER 20

MOVING ON

Some of the POW nurses kept in touch throughout the years. Ethel Thor maintained a number of close friendships. She lived a two-hour drive from Charlie Dworsky, and once a year the women and their children visited. At those times Ethel's daughters, Linda, Carla, and Sandy, might overhear some talk about the women's time in the Philippines.

"She was quiet and a very private person," says Carla. She and her sisters pieced together their mother's story bit by bit. For instance, one day the rice for dinner burned and stuck in the bottom of the pan, and Ethel told her daughters, "In the camp that crusty part on the bottom of the pan was like candy."

"It's sad. Looking back, we didn't really know her as a person," Linda Bradley says. "If we'd ask her questions, she'd say yes or no. But no details. If you asked her something and it made her cry, you didn't ask her again."

Linda believes the POW nurses thought that if family members heard what had happened to them during the war, either they wouldn't believe it, or they'd be horrified. Neither option could be borne.

In 1991, Ethel told a reporter, "I've never talked to anyone about it. I guess I saw so many who lost their lives—I feel it isn't right for me to be sitting here now."

The nurses' memories of leaving their patients on Bataan remained painful through the years. "Those eyes just followed us," Army Nurse Minnie Breese remembered.

"Walking out in the middle of an operation with hundreds lined up under the trees waiting for surgery was devastating to me," said Lucy Wilson Jopling. "This I have to live with for the rest of my life."

JOSIE NESBIT SEEMED TO FIND PEACE ABOUT her wartime hardships. "Being a 'senior' nurse . . . had its myriad responsibilities as well as compensations," she said. "I can assure you, the responsibilities greatly outweighed the compensations, and yet, I would not have had it otherwise.

"The Junior Nurses looked to me for both example and guidance, and it is with great pride I announce I was able to fulfill this duty to the U.S. Army for the duration. . . . I have no rancor, bitterness, envy, or jealousy as to who or whom was selected to leave the combat zone. I knew only that it was my duty to stay with the men who had given so much of themselves in combat."

Josie married Bill Davis, a fellow POW in Santo Tomas. "He still has horrible dreams that they're after him. He won't go out of the house," Josie wrote a friend. Bill returned Josie's support. "I depend on him," she said. "He is my helper and protector."

Through the years, Josie continued to hold the ties that bound her "girls." She remembered their birthdays and Christmas with cards and notes.

Josie remained active and outlived many of the other nurses. She died in 1993 going on ninety-nine years old.

A few of the POW nurses clung to one another throughout the years. "My roommate, in there," Charlie Dworsky said, "we still keep in touch with each other every day of our lives, practically."

Many years after the liberation at Los Baños, Peggy Nash heard that a fellow POW was looking for her. She got in contact and discovered that the POW was Elizabeth, the baby she had carried to freedom.

"To tell the truth, I had forgotten about the baby," Peggy said. Elizabeth had never had a birth certificate. Peggy wrote an affidavit, testifying she had delivered Elizabeth at the camp hospital. From then on, they kept in touch. Peggy saved a letter she received from Elizabeth in 1989.

Thank you so much for the clipping and the photo of yourself. They give substance to what I imagine must have happened in those early days of my life. . . . I realize how lucky I am to be alive, and for that in part I must thank you for your role in protecting me.
Affectionately, Elizabeth

Opposite: Ethel Thor with her husband, Ted Nelson, and daughters (left to right) Carla, Sandy, and Linda on a train trip to Kansas in 1956.

In later years, Peggy volunteered, taking care of sick senior citizens in their homes. She enjoyed telling young students about her personal wartime experiences and was close to her nieces and nephews. One niece decided at ten years old that she wanted to be like Peggy. She later joined the Navy. Peggy outlived all her siblings and died in 1992 at age eighty-one.

Like Peggy, a few of the captive nurses never married, but most of them became wives and mothers, the roles not only expected of them but that they desired. During Frankie Lewey's convalescence after liberation, she was sent to McCloskey General Hospital in Temple, Texas. One of the patients was a first lieutenant learning to get around on one foot. Frankie saw Francis Jerrett's name on a patient list and sought him out. They had met the night Francis lost his foot, the night Frankie had gained her freedom and broken into tears watching over him. The two spent several weeks getting better acquainted and married two months later.

Eventually retired from the Army, Frankie enjoyed being a wife and mother to her daughter, Susan. "When I was in middle school, I realized what she had been through," Susan says. "I had to write a report about starvation, and how starving people had to be introduced to food bite by bite. I knew that she could tell me. Though I wasn't consciously aware of the details, I knew enough to ask her the question."

If Frankie suffered from memories of her time during the war, Susan caught only a glimpse of it—the one time she saw her mother cry.

"I asked her if God graded on a curve," says Susan. "She was at the kitchen stove. She didn't say anything. But she started crying. She grabbed a kitchen towel and came to sit at the table and cried into that towel. Cried for the longest time. Then she turned to me and said, 'I certainly hope not.'"

"Why?" Susan asked her.

"Because if I were to do nothing but good every day for the rest of my life, I could never equal the good those soldiers on Bataan did."

Years later, Frankie told Susan about the wounded soldier on Bataan who had given her his mother's ring and asked her to remember him.

"She tried for years to remember his name, and it never came to her," says Susan. "She was so ashamed of herself . . . she could not recall his name no matter how hard she tried."

Like Frankie, Sally Blaine left the Army and married. Her husband, "Zip" Millet, joined the Army Diplomatic Corps, and the newlyweds moved to Fort Bragg, North Carolina. Sally suffered aching joints from her bouts with malaria and dengue fever and what would today likely be diagnosed as post-traumatic stress disorder.

"I must have been having horrible dreams—I don't remember them—I just know I soaked my nightgown," Sally said of her sweat-drenched nights. Zip was understanding because of his POW experience and calmed her after the nightmares.

Zip became a military attaché, and they moved to Beirut, Lebanon. Later he worked at the American Embassy in Amman, Jordan. As his wife, Sally entertained statesmen and royalty. She presided over elegant dinners at a dining table seating forty people.

They'd been married nine years and had two sons when Zip was diagnosed with leukemia. He died shortly thereafter. "I never cried—I couldn't—there was no time to cry," Sally said. "I had two little boys, and I was afraid that if I started weeping, someone would step in and make all my decisions. I didn't want anybody to do that."

"She was one tough lady," says Van, her older son. "When he died, she earned a degree in political science from Washburn University in hopes of working for the United Nations."

Later Sally served as Director of Nurses at a Topeka nursing school and after that ran a nurses registry in Santa Barbara, California. Single mothers were much less common in those days than they are today. Raising two boys alone, Sally needed the steel she'd tempered during the war.

She instilled in her boys, 'You don't cry. You don't feel sorry for yourself, you forge ahead.' One of her sayings was, 'The sun always comes up in the morning,'" Van says. "She was my role model."

In 1985 Sally retired to San Antonio to live near Van and his family, where she became a minor celebrity. "Her whole life revolved around her wartime experience. It impressed itself upon her more even than her marriage or her children," says Van.

"I never made it to the UN, but I have led a very full life," Sally said. She died at ninety-one.

Rita Palmer's sweetheart, Edwin Nelson, never returned from the war, having died on a prison ship sailing to Japan. Perhaps this loss hurt so much that Rita wanted to leave it behind forever. Throughout her life, she often denied reports that she and Edwin had married on Bataan in the last days of battle.

Leaving the Army, Rita enrolled at the University of Chicago on the GI Bill in February 1946. There she met Lloyd James. Rita had rebelled against the strictures of her New England family, and in Lloyd she met a kindred mind. He had been a labor organizer in the 1930s, and they shared radical political views.

Rita and Lloyd married and raised four children, making an early decision not to tell them about the horrors of her World War II experience. Her youngest daughter, Kathi, discovered the secret when she was eleven and found a box in the attic containing newspaper articles about her mother's past.

"She was a remarkably gentle woman, for what she had been through, and kept her sense of humor," Kathi Mullin says. "She always felt she didn't deserve the Purple Heart."

Rita tried to go back to nursing but became frustrated with protocol that limited which hospital tasks and procedures a nurse could perform. She had a sharp, curious mind and was always reading and keeping up on politics. In her fifties, Rita joined college students demonstrating against the Vietnam War. In later years she and Lloyd quit their jobs and moved to the Sawtooth Mountains of Idaho.

Hattie Brantley, Madeline Ullom, and Rosemary Hogan continued their military careers. Rosemary shifted to the Air Force Nurse Corps, which sprouted from the Army in 1949. She was the fourth American woman to attain the rank of full colonel. Initially, Hattie left the Army to marry a Navy man she'd met in prison camp. They sailed a boat across the Pacific and lived in Panama for a time. Hattie returned to the Army when her thirteen-year marriage ended. Her POW past remained unknown to her colleagues during her active-duty service, which ended in 1969.

At her retirement dinner, "then they realized who I was," she said. Women joining the Army and Navy Nurse Corps did not learn the history of their predecessors' service in World War II.

Hattie moved back to Texas and lived with her brother. When they inherited a hive of bees, Hattie became a beekeeper. She and her brother eventually kept forty hives. "It's a full-time job, but it's kind of fun," she said. Hattie died in September 2006 at age ninety-one.

Madeline Ullom earned both a bachelor and master of science degree and worked in nursing education. On active duty for twenty-eight years, she retired a lieutenant colonel. In retirement Madeline joined efforts to improve benefits for ex-POWs, serving two terms on the Congressional Committee for Veterans Affairs. She became well-known in her local community of Tucson, Arizona, telling her POW story, which she said remained in her thoughts daily.

Madeline remained active for many years in civic, nursing, and veterans' organizations, including the American Defenders of Bataan & Corregidor and American Legion Post 71. She also nursed an artistic flair, taking up oil painting in her later years. Madeline died in 2001 at age ninety.

SIXTEEN OF THE SURVIVING EX-POW ARMY nurses and members of the veterans' group American Defenders of Bataan & Corregidor returned to the Philippines in 1980. They visited the battlefields and prison camps and helped dedicate several memorials. One memorial had been erected to honor the nurses by the men who survived the Bataan Death March. The soldiers dubbed them the Angels of Bataan and Corregidor.

Rita Palmer did not make the trip because she refused to be honored by the Philippines' current militarist regime, led by Ferdinand Marcos. Frankie Lewey didn't go because she believed it would be too painful to relive her memories. Ethel Thor Nelson and Dorothy Scholl Arnold made the trip, each bringing a daughter.

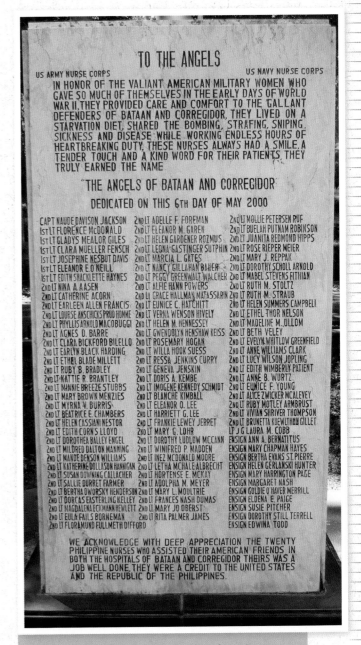

A memorial on Corregidor Island to the U.S. Army nurses who served during the Battle of Bataan and the defense of Corregidor, 1941. The men they served with called them the Angels of Bataan and Corregidor.

"I was stunned walking through the lateral that housed the hospital and sleeping quarters for the nurses on Corregidor," Dorothy's daughter, Carolyn Torrence, said.

Ethel's daughter Linda said, "Going to Santo Tomas was the most emotional day for them, but no tears." They visited the classroom at Santo Tomas where her mother had slept, the Army-Navy club where Ethel had dined and danced, and the site of the Battle of Bataan. "Bataan is no longer a jungle, but more rolling hills and cleared forests, so it was a jungle only in their memories."

"It was so hot walking up to the grounds on Mount Samat, we used an umbrella to keep the sun off of us," Carolyn said. "It dawned on me that the soldiers and nurses had to endure these weather conditions during the war. It made me so proud to be the daughter of one of the Angels."

Dorothy and Harold raised four children. When he died, she lived with Carolyn until passing away in 2000 at age eighty-seven. "I wouldn't want to live it over, but I did learn from it," Dorothy once said of prison camp. "I believe the whole experience helped me. Because of it I learned to accept and to endure."

Above: U.S. Army nurses who served during the 1942 defense of Corregidor revisit the Philippine battlefield where they have been honored with a memorial. Left to right: Anna Williams, Hattie Brantley, Denny Williams, Rose Rieper, Floramund Fellmeth, Willa Hook, Imogene Kennedy, Ann Berntitus, Eunice Young, Verna Hively, Grace Hallman, Dorothy Scholl Arnold, and Ethel Thor Nelson. Not pictured: Sally Blaine Millett and Evelyn Greenfield.

Opposite: Left to right: Lieutenant Colonel Hattie Brantley, Captain Sally Blaine, and Captain Earlyn "Blackie" Black Harding hold the flag that an unknown POW hid until the liberation of the Philippines. Fort Sam Houston Medical Museum, April 21, 1999.

CHAPTER 21
RECOGNITION AT LAST

Today's American military nursing ranks include men as well as women. More than nine thousand Army nurses serve around the globe on active duty. The modern Naval Nurse Corps numbers about 1,500 nurses, including active-duty and reserve nurses. They serve on hospital ships, cruisers, battleships, and aircraft carriers as medevac, intensive care unit (ICU), and even pediatric nurses.

In addition, the number of women in all branches of U.S. military service has dramatically increased since 1973, when the draft ended and American armed forces became all-volunteer. Women are an invaluable and essential part of the military. Today women make up about 14 percent of the active-duty U.S. military.

In early 2013, the Pentagon lifted its 1994 ban on women serving in ground combat units. This historic change opened hundreds of thousands of jobs in infantry, armor, and other previously all-male units. It also made women's service in combat official, acknowledging their contributions and sacrifices. For more than a decade of war in Afghanistan and Iraq, women

Above: Former POW Dorothy Scholl Armold meets president Ronald Reagan during a National POW/MIA Recognition Day Ceremony at the White House, 1983.

Right: On a hill rising from Corregidor Island stands the Monument of the Eternal Flame. This dynamic steel sculpture, located behind the Pacific War Memorial Dome of Peace, sits on a raised platform above a reflecting pool. Designed by Aristides Demetrios, the sculpture commemorates the sacrifices and struggle by the United States and the Philippines to preserve the freedom of future generations.

have risked their lives, serving ably under fire, more than 150 of them perishing. Ultimately, women could potentially be allowed to serve in elite special-operations units, including the Army's Delta Force and the Navy's SEALs.

The service and sacrifice of the World War II Army and Navy POW nurses, however, largely slipped through the cracks of history and was mostly forgotten. Many of the sixty-seven POW nurses written about in this book had died by

1983, when the group was belatedly honored at a National POW/MIA Recognition Day at the White House with President Ronald Reagan. Thirty-one nurses were able to attend the event, including Ethel, Hattie, Carolyn, Madeline, Peggy, and Dorothy. It was the largest group of these POW nurses to gather since 1945.

In a tribute long past due, Major Maude Campbell Davison, commander of the POW Army nurses, was awarded posthumously the Distinguished Service Medal on August 20,

2001, at the Women in Military Service for America Memorial, located at the Ceremonial Entrance to Arlington National Cemetery.

While history may have forgotten these women, unfortunately the terrors of war and prison camps revisited a number of the POW nurses as they neared the end of their lives. Ethel Thor's daughters said anxiety and fear of imagined danger haunted their mother's last months of life.

Eleanor Garen feared that bombs were dropping on her nursing home. She hid food, worrying that the staff would steal it. She mumbled about buckets of blood and tunnels.

Susan Sacharski, the archivist at Northwestern Memorial Hospital, met Eleanor in the early 1990s. "She had the sweetest smile; her whole face lit up," Susan said. "But she struggled emotionally, though she wasn't one to complain. Her health was failing . . . and near the end her flashbacks became more pronounced."

Mildred Dalton Manning, the last living POW nurse, died March 8, 2013, at age ninety-eight. Reminders of her wartime experiences remained constant up until her death. "I cut clothes off so many soldiers that, to this day, if I use scissors, I get a blister."

She trembled describing the day over seventy years ago that the Japanese bombed Clark Field. "It was terrible." She shook her head. "I was scared from the day the war started until the day I came home. . . . And even now I still have anxiety. It never leaves you. You just go on doing what you have to do every day."

Still, "I never looked back," Millie said. "I try not to think about the bad stuff."

But some memories stick in the mind forever.

"The day the war started, I was getting fitted for a pair of riding boots. I was learning to ride . . . going to do all these wonderful things . . . see the Orient," remembered Millie. "I saw a little bit of Manila. I saw Bataan and Corregidor. I saw the war. I saw the inside of a prison camp. That was as far as I got. I never did learn to ride."

Millie shared the attitude of many of the POW nurses. "I was just a nurse doing my duty. But it does leave you impatient with people who complain."

Millie and the other women had enlisted to serve as Army and Navy nurses in part because it was their nature to give of themselves and care for others. Yet likely they did not seek a great test of courage or yearn to sacrifice years of their life and health. Rather, they would have had the same desires and dreams of many young women today—to be independent, to have fun, to find love, and to work at something meaningful.

When events much larger than they could control took over their lives, they chose to summon pure grit moment by moment. Amid the suffering and violence of combat and despite personal hardship in prison camps, they continued, day by day, to simply do their best to keep themselves going and to alleviate the pain of others.

This may be the deceptively facile recipe for courage, and possibly it is even evidence that each of us carries the capacity for such grit, should it be demanded of us.

air raid – An attack by military aircraft armed with bombs.

ammunition dump – A storage place for bullets, grenades, bombs, and explosive devices.

amtrac – "Amphibious tractor," a small landing or transport craft adapted for both land and water with continuous tracks, or caterpillar treads, introduced by the U.S. military during World War II. Originally intended as cargo conveyors for ship-to-shore operations, amtracs rapidly evolved into assault-troop and fire-support vehicles as well.

antiaircraft artillery – Large-caliber weapons, such as cannons, howitzers, and missile launchers, that are operated by ground crews to fire at attacking aircraft.

banzai – The Japanese soldiers' battle cry; literally, "[May you live for] ten thousand years." Originally a greeting to the Emperor.

bayonet – A blade fitted on the muzzle end of a rifle and used as a weapon in hand-to-hand combat.

beriberi – A disease caused by a deficiency of thiamine (vitamin B_1), characterized by inflammation of the nerves, loss of muscle function, and heart failure.

blackout – A time during war when all lights in an area are extinguished or covered to hide the location from enemy bombers.

blitzkrieg – From the German word meaning "lighting war," a war tactic used by Nazi Germany in World War II, whereby troops in vehicles, such as tanks, made rapid surprise attacks supported by air strikes. These tactics resulted in the swift German conquest of France in 1940.

Boeing B-17 Flying Fortress – A four-engine, high-flying, long-range heavy bomber airplane developed in the 1930s for the U.S. Army Air Corps, armed with thirteen machine guns to defend itself and able to carry more than three tons of bombs.

chief nurse – Title used during World War II by both the Army and the Navy for the nurse assigned to lead, organize, assign, and evaluate the entire group of lesser-ranked nurses—her nursing staff. The chief nurse collaborated with the "commanding officer," usually a doctor who was in charge of an entire hospital during that war.

commandant – An officer in charge of a particular force or institution.

convoy – A group of ships or vehicles traveling together for mutual protection.

corpsman – A military enlisted person trained to give first aid in combat and carry the wounded from battle.

Curtiss P-40 Warhawk – U.S. single-engine, single-seat, high-speed military airplane designed for air-to-air combat and ground attack.

debridement – The cutting away of dead or contaminated tissue or foreign matter from a wound to aid healing.

dengue fever – A viral disease of the tropics transmitted by mosquitoes and characterized by sudden fever, rash, and aching head and joints.

dog tag – A metal disk worn around the neck by members of the military, identifying them by name and sometimes serial number, blood type, religious affiliation, and the like.

dysentery – Infection of the intestines resulting in pain, fever, fatigue, and severe diarrhea, sometimes with blood and mucus in the feces; amoebic dysentery caused by protozoans, bacillary dysentery caused by bacteria, both transmitted by contaminated food or water and spread by human contact.

ether – A colorless, volatile, highly flammable liquid used as a solvent; formerly used as an anesthetic.

Executive Committee – A group of POWs elected by their peers to govern and make decisions for the internees of Santo Tomas Internment Camp, they served at the whim of the Japanese commandant.

field – Short for "field of battle" in military language; also used when troops practice maneuvers in the "field" during peacetime.

Filipino-American Army – The combined force of Philippine and U.S. troops charged with defense of the Philippine Islands in 1941.

G.I. – Stamped on soldiers' equipment, stood for Government Issue; became nickname for soldiers in World War II.

G.I. Bill – Common name for the U.S. Servicemen's Readjustment Act of 1944; offered government benefits for World War II veterans, including money for tuition and living expenses to attend college or high school or for vocational education.

Great Depression – The economic crisis and business slowdown in the United States and other countries, roughly beginning with the U.S. stock market crash in October 1929, and continuing through most of the 1930s.

The Great War – The name for World War I before World War II.

Hague Conference of 1907 – International peace conference where dozens of countries agreed to rules for just warfare. In part, the rules required humane treatment for prisoners of war; regarding food, clothing, and shelter, nations agreed to treat enemy prisoners as they would their own soldiers.

howitzer – A high-angle cannon with a short barrel that fires shells at high trajectories for a short range, usually larger and heavier than a mortar and loaded from the rear of the barrel.

internee – Civilian prisoner of war, or person detained in a prison (internment) camp for political reasons or on suspicion of terrorism.

Kempeitai – Military police arm of the Japanese Imperial Army, often compared to the German Gestapo.

latrine – A (usually communal) toilet, with or without plumbing.

leper colony – A place where people with leprosy are quarantined; historically, leprosy was a dreaded disease because it caused visible disfigurement and disability, was incurable, and was believed to be highly contagious, though doctors now know that leprosy is not highly infectious and can be treated successfully if diagnosed early.

litter – A stretcher.

malaria – A disease caused by parasites transmitted by mosquitoes, marked by chills and fever.

medic – Corpsman; a military enlisted person who accompanies combat troops into battle to give first aid, carry off the wounded, etc.

mess – Military dining area or service.

morphine – A narcotic used to relieve pain.

mortar – A high-angle cannon with a short barrel that fires shells at high trajectories for a short range. Usually smaller and more portable than howitzers. Muzzle-loaded, meaning the projectile is dropped into the front of the barrel before firing.

navy yard – A shipyard for construction, repair, equipping, or docking of naval vessels.

open city – When an enemy is about to capture a city, the defending military authorities may declare it an open city, thus announcing they have abandoned defense of it and will allow the enemy to march in without resistance. The aim is to protect civilians and property from battle. The rules for an open city were agreed to by dozens of countries at the Hague Conference.

paratrooper – A soldier trained to attack after parachuting from an aircraft.

penicillin – Antibiotic developed from *Penicillium* molds; not widely used for infection until World War II.

peripheral neuropathy – Damage to nerves of the peripheral nervous system (the section of the nervous system lying outside the brain and spinal cord), which may be caused by disease.

post-traumatic stress disorder – Anxiety disorder affecting people who have experienced profound emotional trauma, such as military combat, torture, rape, or a natural disaster; characterized by recurrent flashbacks, nightmares, eating disorders, anxiety, fatigue, forgetfulness, and social withdrawal. Also called post-traumatic stress syndrome.

quinine – A bitter crystalline compound present in cinchona bark, used as a tonic and formerly as an anti-malarial drug.

ration – An amount of food supplied on a regular basis, especially to members of the armed forces during a war.

repatriation – Sending a person back to his or her own country.

sawali – Woven matting of flattened bamboo strips used to make partitions, walls, and baskets; used to construct the indigenous Philippine house called a nipa hut.

scurvy – A disease caused by a deficiency of vitamin C, marked by swollen, bleeding gums and the opening of previously healed wounds.

shell – An explosive artillery projectile.

strafe – Attack repeatedly with machine-gun fire from low-flying aircraft.

sulfa – A drug used in combating certain bacterial infections.

triage – Process for sorting injured people into groups based on their need for or likely benefit from immediate medical treatment; used in hospital emergency rooms, on battlefields, and at disaster sites when limited medical resources must be allocated.

War Plan Orange (WPO) – A series of U.S. Joint Army and Navy Board plans for dealing with a possible attack by Japan during the years between the First and Second World Wars; the final plan, WPO-3, was a strategy for defending the Philippine Islands.

ward – A division in a hospital; a large room in a hospital for the care of patients often requiring similar treatment.

Zero – Mitsubishi A6M Zero; fighter aircraft of the Imperial Japanese Navy combining excellent maneuverability and very long range; considered the most capable carrier-based fighter in the world when introduced early in World War II; by 1943 newer American fighters surpassed the Zero with greater firepower, armor, and speed; the Zero was used in kamikaze (suicide) attacks.

LIST OF NURSES

The following lists contain all the U.S. Military nurses serving in the Philippines when the Japanese invaded the islands, and includes their hometowns when that information was available. Unless designated otherwise, the women all became prisoners of war and were held in Japanese camps. Military titles have been included when that information was available. An asterisk denotes that the individual is discussed in this book. I regret not having been able to include the stories of all these heroic women.

NAVY NURSE CORPS PRISONERS OF WAR

*Commander Laura Mae Cobb, Wichita, Kansas

Mary F. Chapman, Chicago, Illinois

Captain Bertha R. Evans, Portland, Oregon

Helen C. Gorzelanski, Omaha, Nebraska

Mary Rose Harrington, Elk Point, South Dakota

*Commander (honorary) Margaret A. Nash, Wilkes-Barre, Pennsylvania

Lieutenant Commander Goldia "Goldie" A. O'Haver, Hayfield, Minnesota

Eldene E. Paige, Lomita, California

*Lieutenant Commander Susie J. Pitcher, Des Moines, Iowa

*Lieutenant Commander Dorothy Still, Long Beach, California

*Captain Edwina Todd, Pomona, California

ARMY NURSE CORPS PRISONERS OF WAR

*Philippines ANC Commander Major Maude Campbell Davison, Washington, D.C.

*Major Josephine May "Josie" Nesbit, Parlin, Colorado

Captain Mina A. Aasen, Minot, North Dakota

Captain Louise M. Anschicks, Mendota, Illinois

First Lieutenant Phyllis J. Arnold, Minneapolis, Minnesota

Agnes D. Barre, Orange, Texas

First Lieutenant Clara Mae "Bickie" Bickford, Tivoli, Texas

*First Lieutenant Earlyn "Blackie" Black, Groesbeck, Texas

*First Lieutenant Ethel "Sally" L. Blaine, Bible Grove, Missouri

*Colonel Ruby G. Bradley, Spencer, West Virginia

*Lieutenant Colonel Hattie R. Brantley, Jefferson, Texas

*Second Lieutenant Minnie L. Breese, Arlington Heights, Illinois

First Lieutenant Myra V. Burris, San Antonio, Texas

First Lieutenant Helen "Cassie" M. Cassiani, Bridgewater, Massachusetts

*Major Beatrice E. Chambers, Manila, Philippine Islands

Edith M. Corns, Cleveland, Ohio

*First Lieutenant Mildred "Millie" Dalton, Jefferson, Georgia

Kathryn L. Dollason, Augusta, Georgia

*Captain Sallie P. Durrett, Louisville, Kentucky

*Captain Bertha "Charlie" Dworsky, Halletsville, Texas

Dorcas E. Easterling, Abbot, Texas

First Lieutenant Magdalena Eckman, Pine Grove, California

Second Lieutenant Eula R. Fails, Houston, Texas

*Major Adele F. Foreman, Masten, Pennsylvania

First Lieutenant Earleen Allen, Chicago, Illinois

First Lieutenant Helen L. Gardner, Aberdeen, Ohio

*Major Eleanor Mae Garen, South Bend, Indiana

First Lieutenant Marcia L. Gates, Janesville, Wisconsin

First Lieutenant Beulah M. "Peggy" Greenwalt, Seattle, Washington

First Lieutenant Alice J. Hahn, Chicago, Illinois

Lieutenant Colonel Helen M. Hennessey, Leavenworth, Kansas

Captain Gwendolyn L. Henshaw, Los Angeles, California

First Lieutenant Verna V. Henson, Trinity, Texas

*Colonel Rosemary Hogan, Chattanooga, Oklahoma

First Lieutenant Geneva Jenkins, Sevierville, Tennessee

Colonel Doris A. Kehoe, Pacific Grove, California

*First Lieutenant Imogene "Jeanne" Kennedy, Philadelphia, Mississippi

First Lieutenant Blanche Kimball, Topeka, Kansas

Eleanor O. Lee, Lonaconing, Maryland

*First Lieutenant Frankie T. Lewey, Dalhart, Texas

Captain Dorothy L. Ludlow, Little Rock, Arkansas

*Inez V. McDonald, Tupelo, Mississippi

First Lieutenant Letha McHale, Haverhill, Massachusetts

Lieutenant Colonel Winifred P. Madden, Montello, Wisconsin

*Captain Gladys Ann Mealor, Gorgas, Alabama

Mary Brown Menzie, New Orleans, Louisiana

Adolpha M. Meyer, St. Louis, Missouri

Captain Clara L. Mueller, Philadelphia, Pennsylvania

*Major Frances Louise Nash, Washington, Georgia

Captain Mary J. Oberst, Owensboro, Kentucky

Captain Eleanor "Peg" O'Neill, Providence, Rhode Island

*First Lieutenant Rita G. Palmer, Hampton, New Hampshire

First Lieutenant Beulah M. Putnam, Worthington, Ohio

Major Mary J. Reppak, Shelton, Connecticut

Major Rose F. Rieper, St. Louis, Missouri

*First Lieutenant Dorothy Scholl, Independence, Missouri

Lieutenant Colonel Edith E. "Shack" Shacklette, Brandenberg, Kentucky

Ruth M. Stoltz, Dayton, Ohio

*First Lieutenant Ethel M. Thor, Tacoma, Washington

*Lieutenant Colonel Madeline M. Ullom, O'Neill, Nebraska

*First Lieutenant Evelyn B. Whitlow, Leasburg, North Carolina

*First Lieutenant Anna E. Williams, Harrisburg, Pennsylvania

*Lieutenant Colonel Maude "Denny" Denson Williams, nurse-anesthetist (retired prior to war, evacuated to Bataan, reenlisted)

Lieutenant Colonel Edith M. Wimberly, Campti, Louisiana

First Lieutenant Anne B. Wurts, Leominster, Massachusetts

Lieutenant Colonel Eunice Young, Arkport, New York

*Alice M. "Swish" Zwicker, Brownsville, Maine

ARMY NURSES EVACUATED FROM CORREGIDOR BEFORE SURRENDER

Catherine M. Acorn

Dorothea M. Daley, Hamilton, Missouri

*Floramund A. Fellmeth, Chicago, Illinois (sailed on hospital ship to Australia, December 1941)

Leona Castinger, Alabama

Susan Downing Gallagher

Nancy J. Gillahan

Grace D. Hallman, Georgia

Lieutenant Eunice C. Hatchitt, Prairie Lea, Texas

Willa Hook, Refrow, Oklahoma

Ressa Jenkins, Sevierville, Tennessee

Harriet G. Lee, Boston, Massachusetts

Mary G. Lohr, Greensburg, Pennsylvania

Florence MacDonald, Brockton, Massachusetts

Lieutenant Colonel Hortense McKay, Amherst, Minnesota

Mary L. Moultrie, Georgia

Mollie A. Peterson, Arkansas

*Major Juanita Redmond, Swansea, South Carolina

Mabel V. Stevens, Nebraska

*Ruth W. Straub, Milwaukee, Wisconsin

Helen Summers, Queens, New York

Beth A. Veley, San Jose, California

*Captain Lucy Wilson, Big Sandy, Texas

NAVY NURSE EVACUATED FROM CORREGIDOR BEFORE SURRENDER

Captain Ann Bernatitus, Exeter, Pennsylvania

SELECT TIMELINE

This timeline covers the events preceding World War II and focuses primarily on the war in the Pacific. Events of the war in Europe are noted in italics.

1898 Spanish-American War ends. Philippine Islands ceded by Spain to the United States in Treaty of Paris.

1904-1905 Joint U.S. Army-Navy Board considers possible war with Japan and adopts War Plan Orange (WPO) with the assumption the Philippines would be Japan's first wartime objective.

1921-1924 U.S. military revisions of WPO review America's unfavorable strategic position and recognize Japan as the probable enemy.

1935 General Douglas MacArthur assigned to develop Philippine Army.

1938

September *Munich Agreement between British Prime Minister Neville Chamberlain and German Chancellor (Führer) Adolf Hitler.*

Joint Army-Navy revision of WPO tacitly recognizes the hopeless position of the American forces in the Philippines.

1939

September 1 *Germany invades Poland, World War II begins in Europe.*

September 5 *United States declares neutrality in the European war.*

1940

May 10 *Hitler launches blitzkrieg*

against Holland and Belgium; both countries occupied by Germans.

June 14 *German soldiers march into Paris.*

July 10 *Battle of Britain begins.*

July Army Nurses Ethel Thor, Madeline Ullom, and Juanita Redmond arrive in Manila.

1941

June Hattie Brantley arrives in the Philippines, reports to Fort Stotsenberg Station Hospital.

July Frankie Lewey arrives in Manila.

General Douglas MacArthur named to command U.S. forces in the Far East.

October Hideki Tojo becomes Prime Minister of Japan.

December 7 Japanese bomb Pearl Harbor.

December 8 Japanese attack Philippines at Camp John Hay and Clark Field. United States and Britain declare war on Japan. Japanese land near Singapore and enter Thailand.

December 10 Japanese seize Guam and attack Cavite Naval Shipyard and Cañacao Naval Hospital.

December 12 Japanese land at Legazpi on southern Luzon.

December 18 Japanese invade Hong Kong.

December 22 Japanese come ashore at Lingayen Gulf north of Manila.

December 23 General Douglas MacArthur begins a withdrawal from Manila to Bataan.

December 24 Army nurses begin retreat to Bataan.

December 25 British surrender Hong Kong to Japanese.

December 26 Manila declared an open city.

1942

January 2 Manila and U.S. naval base at Cavite captured by the Japanese. Eleven Navy nurses, including Peggy Nash, taken prisoner.

January 18 *German-Japanese-Italian military agreement signed in Berlin.*

February 15 British surrender to Japanese at Singapore.

February 23 First Japanese attack on the U.S. mainland as a submarine shells an oil refinery near Santa Barbara, California.

March 1 Japanese naval victory in the Battle of the Java Sea as the largest U.S. warship in the Far East, the *Houston*, is sunk.

March 8 Navy nurses taken from Santa Scholastica to Santo Tomas Internment Camp.

March 11 General MacArthur leaves Corregidor for Australia. General Jonathan Wainwright takes over for MacArthur as the new U.S. commander in the Philippines.

April 8-9 Army nurses on Bataan evacuate to Corregidor.

April 9 U.S. forces on Bataan surrender unconditionally to the Japanese. At seventy-eight thousand men (Filipinos and Americans), it is the largest American army in history to surrender.

April 29 Twenty Army nurses evacuate from Corregidor on two seaplanes and stop for refueling on Mindanao. One plane damaged on takeoff strands ten Army nurses. One plane reaches and lands in Australia.

May 3 Submarine *Spearfish* carries eleven Army nurses away from Corregidor.

May 4–8 Japan suffers its first defeat of the war during the Battle of the Coral Sea off New Guinea, the first time in history two opposing aircraft-carrier forces battle with airplanes, the opposing ships never sighting each other.

May 6 Corregidor falls as General Wainwright unconditionally surrenders all U.S. and Filipino forces in the Philippines.

May 10 Ten nurses on Mindanao Island surrender.

May 12 The last U.S. troops holding out in the Philippines surrender on Mindanao.

June 4–7 A turning point in the war when the United States wins a decisive victory against Japan in the Battle of Midway.

July 2 Army nurses taken from Corregidor to Santo Tomas Internment Camp in Manila.

August 8 U.S. Marines take Henderson Field on Guadalcanal. Japan begins to give ground in the war.

September 9 Ten Army nurses arrive at Santo Tomas from Mindanao.

December 31 Japanese troops withdraw from Guadalcanal after five months of bloody fighting against U.S. forces.

1943

U.S. troops begin doggedly taking back ground from the Japanese in the Far East, and battle island by island in the South Pacific.

May 14 Eleven Navy nurses move to Los Baños.

September 8 *Italy surrenders unconditionally to the Allies; German forces rushed to Italy.*

1944

January Japanese military relieves civilian command of Santo Tomas Internment Camp.

March 4 *Allies launch first major daylight air raid on Berlin.*

June 6 *D-Day, Allies invade Normandy, France.*

July 27 American troops liberate Guam.

September 21 U.S. pilots bomb Manila.

October 11 United States flies air raids against Okinawa, Japan.

October 20 U.S. Sixth Army invades Leyte in the Philippines.

October 23–26 U.S. Navy wins a decisive victory over Japan in the Battle of Leyte Gulf, one of the largest naval battles in history.

November 18 *U.S. Third Army crosses the German frontier.*

December 16 *The Battle of the Bulge begins as Germany launches its final offensive through the Ardennes region of Belgium.*

December 17 The U.S. Army Air Corps begin preparations for dropping the atomic bomb on Japan.

1945

January U.S. Army and Navy commands prepare for invasion of Iwo Jima, Okinawa, and Japanese mainland.

January 9 U.S. Sixth Army invades Lingayen Gulf on Luzon in the Philippines.

January 25 *Allied forces prevail in the Battle of the Bulge.*

January 26 *Soviet troops liberate Auschwitz death camp in Poland.*

February 3 U.S. troops liberate Santo Tomas Internment Camp, freeing Army nurses.

February 12 Sixty-five Army nurses leave Santo Tomas Internment Camp for 126th General Hospital on Leyte Island.

February 16 U.S. forces recapture Bataan.

February 23 U.S. Marines raise flag atop Mount Suribachi on Iwo Jima.

U.S. Army Rangers liberate Los Baños Prison Camp and free Navy nurses.

February 24 Army nurses arrive in San Francisco, California.

March 2 U.S. airborne troops recapture Corregidor.

March 3 U.S. and Filipino troops take Manila.

March 9 U.S. bombing raids on Tokyo destroy sixteen square miles of the city and kill an estimated one hundred thousand people.

March 10 U.S. Navy nurses arrive in California.

April 1 U.S. troops land on Okinawa.

April 2 President Franklin Roosevelt dies of a cerebral hemorrhage; Vice President Harry Truman becomes president.

May 8 *Germany surrenders, Victory-in-Europe Day (V-E Day) proclaimed.*

June 28 MacArthur's headquarters announces the end of all Japanese resistance in the Philippines.

July 5 Liberation of Philippines declared.

August 6 First atomic bomb dropped on Hiroshima, Japan.

August 9 Second atomic bomb is dropped on Nagasaki, Japan.

August 14 Japanese accept unconditional surrender; General MacArthur is appointed to head the occupation forces in Japan.

August 16 General Wainwright, a POW since May 6, 1942, is released from a prison camp in Manchuria.

ENDNOTES

CHAPTER 1: ADVENTURE AND ROMANCE

Page 12: "Each evening . . . long dresses": Earlyn Black Harding, Department of Defense (DOD) interview, Washington, D.C., April 9, 1983, 2.

Page 14: "There was no way . . . prepared for war": Mildred (Millie) Manning Dalton, Women in Military Service to America Memorial Foundation, Inc., (WMSAMF) Oral History Collection (OHC) interview, January 29, 2008.

Page 14: "Ed was the executive . . . a ball" and all Peggy Nash quotes in Chapter 1: *The Saga of Margaret Nash, WWII POW* (WMSAMF), Women's Memorial Foundation (WMC), transcription of interview, Arlington, VA, 1.

Page 16: "We were in a strange . . . second thought": Rita Palmer James, Army Nurse Corps (ANC) Oral History interview, Stanley, ID, June 5–6, 1984, 7.

CHAPTER 2: SURPRISE ATTACK

Page 17: "Wake up! No . . ." conversation on news of Pearl Harbor: Dorothy Still Danner, *What a Way to Spend a War: Navy Nurse POWs in the Philippines* (Annapolis, MD: Naval Institute Press, 1995), 30–31.

Page 18: "There were thirty-seven . . . more casualties": Ruby G. Bradley, ANC interview, September 19, 1984, 8.

Page 18: "Girls! Girls! . . . work tonight": Josephine Nesbit Davis, DOD interview, Bolling Air Force Base, Washington, D.C., April 9, 1983.

Page 19: "I'll die before I wear these": Evelyn M. Monahan and Rosemary Neidel-Greenlee, *All This Hell: U.S. Nurses Imprisoned by the Japanese* (Lex-

ington: University of Kentucky Press, 2003), 22.

CHAPTER 3: NO TIME FOR FEAR

Page 22: "Girls, we're at war . . . yours well": Juanita Redmond, *I Served on Bataan* (Philadelphia: L.B. Lippincott Company, 1943), 19.

Page 22: "I often slept . . . to sleep": Madeline Ullom, DOD interview, April 9, 1983, 13.

Page 23: "other disgusting things for people" and on Frances Nash: Evelyn M. Monahan and Rosemary Neidel-Greenlee, *And If I Perish: Frontline U.S. Army Nurses in World War II* (New York: Anchor Books, 2003), 8–19.

Page 25: "It was amazing . . . already dead": Diane Burke Fessler, *No Time for Fear: Voices of American Military Nurses in World War II* (East Lansing: Michigan State University Press, 1996), 80.

Page 25: "Could I have . . . killed me": CMD Margaret "Peggy" Nash, NC (Ret), interview by Andree Marechal-Workman, Oakland Naval Hospital Public Affairs (ONHPA), September 10, 1992, transcript, 3, WMSAMF, WMC.

Page 25: "The next time . . . was burning": Fessler, *No Time for Fear*, 80.

Page 25: "I thought to myself . . . mine included": *The Saga of Margaret Nash*, 2.

Page 25: "It was like a nightmare . . . no time for fear": Fessler, *No Time for Fear*, 80.

CHAPTER 4: NURSES UNDER FIRE

Page 26: "Our planes brought . . . one afternoon": Redmond, *I Served on Bataan*, 23.

Page 27: "I couldn't have . . . had tried": Carolyn A. Torrence, author phone interview, September 9, 2011.

Page 27: "Everybody knows chances . . . beforehand": John A. Glusman, *Conduct Under Fire: Four American Doctors and Their Fight for Life as Prisoners of the Japanese, 1941–1945* (New York: Viking, Penguin Group, 2005), 76.

Page 28: "Girls, pack your . . . heard of Bataan": Lieutenant Colonel H.R. Brantley, USA (Ret), DOD interview, April 9, 1983, 15.

Page 28: "conferences and arguments . . . and protracted": Redmond, *I Served on Bataan*, 28.

Page 29: "If ever there is a war . . . thick of it" and on Frankie Lewey: Susan Jerrett Trout, author interviews, September 7, 2010; November 11, 2011; April 15, 2012, Kirkland, WA.

CHAPTER 5: RETREAT TO THE JUNGLE

Page 31: "to call it a hospital . . . a hotel": Glusman, *Conduct Under Fire*, 77.

Page 32: All Madeline Ullom quotes Chapter 5: Ullom, 11.

Page 32: "Prepare yourself . . ." and further conversation: Monahan, *All This Hell*, 30.

Page 33: "You live a million . . . a foxhole" and on Frances Nash's evacuation to Bataan: Monahan, *And If I Perish*, 16–17.

Page 34: "At least by tomorrow": Monahan, *All This Hell*, 39.

Page 34: "Anything the ambulances . . . to us": Monahan, *All This Hell*, 76.

Page 34: "Despite the confusion . . . her hand": Alfred A. Weinstein, M.D., *Barbed-Wire Surgeon* (New York: The Macmillan Company, 1950), 16.

Page 34: "I give to . . . that pledge": Address to the People of the Philippines on Post-War Independence, August 12, 1943. www.presidency.ucsb.edu/ws/?pid=16443#axzz1iWEsQQif, accessed February 19, 2013.

Page 35: "I'd get down . . . next cot": Monahan, *All This Hell*, 43.

Page 35: "The needles had . . . dissolve the morphine": Brantley, DOD interview, 8.

Page 36: "We evidenced . . . with disbelief": Monahan, *All This Hell*, 39.

Page 37: "We didn't sign it": Peggy Nash, interview, 3.

CHAPTER 6: MAKE-DO MEDICINE

Page 39: "We had a tent . . . the records": Elizabeth M. Norman, *We Band of Angels: The Untold Story of American Nurses Trapped on Bataan by the Japanese* (New York: Random House, 1999), 43.

Page 39: "We sat down . . . and sand" and "I cried at first . . . talk about it" and "Women had a hard time . . . my kitchen": "Bataan Nurse Describes Hospital No. 2 Drama," *Post News* magazine, Fort Sam Houston, TX, 1992. WMSAMF, WMC, no date or page available.

Page 40: "Help is on the way . . . is possible": Norman, *We Band of Angels*, 36–37.

Page 40: "the skies . . . your heads": Denny Williams, *To the Angels* (San Francisco: Denson Press, 1985), 56.

Page 40: "We were the first nurses . . . rear areas": Josephine Nesbit Davis, Maj. ANC, to Dorothy L. Starbuck, Chief Benefits Director, Veterans Administration, January 15, 1983, 2. Courtesy American Defenders of Bataan & Corregidor, Inc.

Page 40: "The first time . . . my patients": Norman, *We Band of Angels*, 77.

Page 41: "Did you hear . . . disaster here": Williams, *To the Angels*, 51.

Page 42: "There's not much . . ." and further Millie Dalton Manning quotes in Chapter 6: WMSAMF, WMC interview #1117.

Page 43: "I finally said . . . need quinine": "Bataan Nurse Describes Hospital No. 2 Drama."

Page 44: "going back to Civil War times": Phyllis Arnold Adams, ANC interview, 14.

Page 44: "Hello folks . . .": Ethel Thor's letters home, courtesy Sandy Thor, Seattle, Washington.

Page 44: "Don't kill me . . .": Anecdote told by Redmond, *I Served on Bataan*, 49.

Page 45: All entries from Ruth Straub's diary in Chapter 6: Norman, *We Band of Angels*, 56–57.

Page 46: "Mostly, you were scared . . . my bed": Millie Dalton Manning, author interview, January 29, 2012, Trenton, NJ.

Page 46: "In the jungle . . . would laugh": Maxine K. Russell, ed., *Jungle Angel: Bataan Remembered: The Testimony of Hortense E. McKay to Maxine K. Russell* (Brainerd, MN: Bang Printing Company, 1988), 33.

Page 46: "FDR said . . . of planes": Williams, *To the Angels*, 66.

CHAPTER 7: BOXED IN ON BATAAN

Pages 47–48: Entry from Lieutenant John P. Burns diary: William H. Barsch, *I Wonder at Times How We Keep Going Here: The 1941–42 Philippines Diary Of Lt. John P. Burns, 21st Pursuit Squadron*. www.highbeam.com/doc/1G1-157097840.html, accessed April 4, 2013.

Page 48: "The President . . . shall return": Edward T. Imparato, *General MacArthur Speeches & Reports: 1908–1964* (New York: Turner Publishing Company, 2000), 124.

Page 48: "I am going to the latrine . . ." and "Dugout Doug's not . . .": Glusman, *Conduct Under Fire*, 131.

Page 49: "You put a rock . . . is tender": William E. Dyess, Lieutenant Colonel, *Bataan Death March: A Survivor's Account* (Lincoln: University of Nebraska Press, 2002), xxix.

Page 49: Ethel Thor's letter, courtesy Sandy Thor.

Page 50: "We've got to . . . won't complain": Edith Shacklette quoted in Redmond, *I Served on Bataan*, 100.

Page 50: "Lately I have been . . . dead men": Monahan, *All This Hell*, 75.

Page 50: "What'll happen to us . . . make it": Redmond, *I Served on Bataan*, 103.

Page 50: "Most of us followed . . . be told": Weinstein, *Barbed-Wire Surgeon*, 34.

Page 50: "The battle was so close . . . gave up": Williams, *To the Angels*, 71–72.

Page 51: "I remember coming to . . . legs, too": Palmer James, 20.

Page 51: "This is the end . . . to identify": Redmond, *I Served on Bataan*, 97.

Page 52: "One of the wards hit . . . wasn't frightened" and "I never went back again . . . be next": Monahan, *All This Hell*, 59.

Page 52: "I'll never forget . . . and dirt": Anna E. Williams Clark, DOD interview, Bolling Air Force Base, Washington, D.C., April 9, 1983, 14.

Page 52: "Quit worrying . . . what comes": Nesbit Davis interview.

CHAPTER 8: RETREAT TO THE ROCK

Page 53: "Hell, it'll have . . . bamboo sticks": Williams, *To the Angels*, 76.

Page 53: "Tell your American nurses . . ." and further conversation with Colonel James O. Gillespie and Nesbit in Chapter 8: Nesbit interview.

Page 54: "We're leaving" and Denny Williams conversation with Bill Williams: Williams, *To the Angels*, 77.

Page 55: All Frankie Lewey quotes in Chapter 8: Trout, interview.

Pages 56–57: On Sally Blaine evacuating Bataan: Norman, *We Band of Angels*, 89.

Page 57: "There wasn't anything . . . and moan": Williams Clark, interview, 15.

Page 57: "My God, look at them": Russel, *Jungle Angel*, 35.

Page 57: "The fact we . . . a miracle": Brantley, DOD interview, 22.

Page 57: "So I lay down . . . that exhausted": Dalton Manning, author interview.

CHAPTER 9: HOLING UP ON CORREGIDOR ISLAND

Page 58: On numbers of nurses: One ANC nurse, Floramund Fellmeth, evacuated Manila December 1941 with wounded on the hospital ship *Mactan*. Denny Williams, retired ANC, returned to Army nursing when the war started, remained on duty throughout the war, and reenlisted. One Navy nurse, Ann Bernatitus, retreated to Bataan with the Army Medical Corps, evacuated to Corregidor, and later evacuated to the United States on the submarine *Spearfish*.

Page 60: "It was like being . . . feel it": Lieutenant Colonel Hattie Brantley interview by Warren Knox, Retired Army Nurse Corps Association Convention, April 28, 1980, San Antonio, TX, 1.

Pages 61–62: All quotes on April 25 attack: Redmond, *I Served on Bataan*, 145–146.

Page 62: "It's a strange thing . . . for pettiness": Zwicker's diary, 7, courtesy Rod Tenny.

CHAPTER 10: RESCUED!

Page 63: "I couldn't see . . . wounded people": Mealor Giles, interview, 18.

Page 64: "I wanted to go . . . a deserter": Redmond, *I Served on Bataan*, 150.

Page 64: All Evelyn Whitlow and Sally Blaine quotes in Chapter 10: *Reminiscences of Two Former P.O.W. Army Nurses in World War II*, interview, March 2, 1983, WMSAMF, WMC, #1875, 2–12.

Page 65: "Why them? . . . the trauma . . .": Norman, *We Band of Angels*, 105.

Page 65: "Sometimes there was . . . often neither": Cabot Coville, "Our Two Months on Corregidor," *The Saturday Evening Post* (June 27, 1942), 102.

Page 65: "This morning I sat . . ." and all further quotes: Zwicker's diary, 2–3.

Page 65: "Situation here . . . desperate": Louis Morton, *The War in the Pacific: The Fall of the Philippines* (Washington, D.C.: Center for Military History, Government Printing Office, 1953), 548.

Page 65: "I couldn't write . . . to say?": Hattie Brantley, oral interview by Cindy Weigland, June 5, 2002, WMSAMF, WMC, #11267.

Page 66: On outnumbering them twenty-one to one: Glusman, *Conduct Under Fire*, 183.

Page 67: "Now our facial . . . and brave": Williams, *To the Angels*, 96.

CHAPTER 11: SURRENDER TO THE ENEMY

Page 68: "Under New Management": Mary Oberst, ANC, quoted by Lawrence Keith, "An 'Angel of Bataan,'" *Owensboro Message-Inquirer*, 2A. WMFC, #1357.

Page 68: "This was . . . OF NANKING": Nesbit Davis, to Starbuck, 3–4.

Page 68: "I was scared spitless": Inez McDonald Moore, ANC interview, Bolling Air Force Base, Washington, D.C., April 9, 1983.

Page 69: "We kept taking care . . . those things" and all Brantley quotes in Chapter 11: Brantley, DOD interview, 25–31.

Page 69: "They lined us up . . . your universities" and all Ullom quotes in Chapter 11: DOD interview, 21–24.

Page 69: "They looked us up . . . scared her": Dalton Manning, WMC interview.

Page 72: "After climbing that . . . of bridge": Williams, *To the Angels*, 119.

CHAPTER 12: HELD INCOMMUNICADO

Page 74: "No talking!": Williams, *To the Angels*, 123.

Page 74: "their first fresh fruit in six months": Ethel Thor diary, courtesy Sandy Thor.

Page 74: "Somebody with . . . get off": Brantley WMC interview.

Page 74: "They discussed us . . . YOUR EYES": Williams, *To the Angels*, 124.

Page 75: "They wanted us . . . about it": Brantley, DOD interview, 29.

Page 75: "We thought we . . . of the soldiers": Bradley, interview, 20.

Page 75: "We had three showers . . . using that": Ullom, interview, 32.

Page 76: "And my mattress . . . those slats": Brantley, WMC interview.

Page 78: "We reasoned . . . Army Nurses": Nesbit Davis to Starbuck, 3.

Page 78: "I think the . . . all the time" and "we never knew . . . all times": Peggy Nash, interview, 4.

Page 79: All Blaine and Whitlow quotes in Chapter 12: *Reminiscences of Two Former P.O.W. Army Nurses in World War II*, 10.

CHAPTER 13: SANTO TOMAS INTERNMENT CAMP

Page 80: "You knew something must be going on!": Bertha Dworsky Henderson, DOD interview, 18.

Page 81: "She saved our lives": WMFC, #11267.

Page 81: "From time to time . . . the nurses": Nesbit Davis to Starbuck, 3.

Page 81: "Our group was . . . camp garden": Ada N. Hayes, "Three Years in a Prison Camp," *Hampton Union*, May 10, 1945. http://www .hampton.lib.nh.us/hampton/biog/ ritapalmer/3yearsinaprisoncamp.htm, accessed February 11, 2013.

Page 82: "You could read . . ." and "All day it was a . . .": Brantley DOD interview, 33.

Page 82: "If anyone escaped . . . if you do": Peggy Nash, interview, 4.

Pages 82–83: Frances Nash conversation with doctor: Monahan, *All This Hell*, 122.

Page 83: "Great mental . . . inane conversation": Williams, *To the Angels*, 146.

Pages 83–84: "It was hard . . . amazing women": Sascha Weinzheimer, author phone interview, August 21, 2012.

Page 84: U.S. War Department letter, courtesy Sandy Thor.

Pages 84–85: "Your sister, Ethel . . . she doesn't grumble": Corregidor evacuee Susan Downing Gallagher to Vivian Johnson, June 13, 1943, courtesy Sandy Thor.

Page 85: "I must be allergic": Danner, *What a Way to Spend a War*, 122.

Pages 85–86: "We were all crying" and all further Peggy Nash quotes in Chapter 13: *The Saga of Margaret Nash*, 8–9.

CHAPTER 14: FOOD? GROW YOUR OWN

Page 87: "Bakis were worn . . . to the feet": Hayes, "Three Years in a Prison Camp."

Pages 87–90: "When your underwear . . . on them" and "I knew a Dutch . . . in the rice": WMFC interview.

Pages 88–89: "I have found that . . . are victorious": Eva Anna Nixon, *Delayed Manila* (Newberg, OR: Friendsview Manor, 1981), 59.

Page 89: "If you want . . . have a garden" and all Eva Nixon quotes in Chapter 14: Nixon, *Delayed Manila*, 61–62.

Page 89: "It took every . . . that was that" and all further Josephine Nesbit quotes in Chapter 14: Nesbit Davis to Starbuck, 4. Josie speaks of sixty-eight nurses, which include ANC nurses Ruby Bradley and Beatrice Chambers, who were captured at Baguio at the start of the war and later brought to Santo Tomas to join the others.

Page 90: "We traded lots . . . look better": *Reminiscences of Two Former P.O.W. Army Nurses in World War II*, 21.

Page 91: "Occasionally they could . . . the camp": J. C. Martin, "A Christmas Present Nurse Will Never Forget," *The Arizona Daily Star* (December 25, 1977). WMSAMF, WMC, Madeline M. Ullom Collection, #2118.

Page 91: "They would toss . . . hungry children" and "It was surprising how well it tasted": Hayes, "Three Years in a Prison Camp."

Page 91: "delegated a girl . . . could find": Williams, *To the Angels*, 186.

Page 91: "It had potatoes . . . over again . . ." and "A strange kind . . . the camp": Norman, *We Band of Angels*, 195.

Page 92: "Do you not realize . . . it's fun": Nixon, *Delayed Manila*, 70.

Page 92: "I couldn't believe . . . opened fire": Williams, *To the Angels*, 193.

CHAPTER 15: HOPE AT LAST

Page 93: "They're Americans . . . ours": Williams, *To The Angels*, 193.

Pages 93–94: "Look at that . . . it beautiful": Tressa R. Cates, R.N., *The Drainpipe Diary* (New York: Vantage Press, 1957), 219.

Page 94: "They'd wake us . . . to you": Dalton Manning, author interview.

Page 95: "We would have . . . for hours": Monahan, *All This Hell*, 133.

Page 95: "It may have . . . gradually disappeared": Hayes, "Three Years in a Prison Camp."

Page 95: "Two hundred ducks . . . starving, too": A. V. Hartendorf, *The Santo Tomas Story, Edited from the Official History of the Santo Tomas Internment Camp by F. H. Golay* (New York: McGraw-Hill, 1964), 329.

Page 96: "wallpaper paste" and further Peggy Nash quotes on food: ONHPA interview, 4–5.

Page 96: "We kept taking . . ." and all further Peggy Nash quotes in Chapter 15: *The Saga of Margaret Nash, WWII POW*, 11–12.

CHAPTER 16: WALKING SKELETONS

Pages 97–98: "We had to laugh . . . us cry": Sears, Barbara, *Tucsonan Will Observe Corregidor Anniversary*, WMSAMF, MFC, #2118.

Page 98: "Their eyes gradually . . . shoulders drooped . . .": Josephine Nesbit, *History of the Army Nurse Corps in the Philippine Islands, September 1949–February 1945*. Unpublished manuscript, (AMEDD), 43.

Page 98: "I'd wake up . . . other people" and "We've got to have . . . these girls": Norman, *We Band of Angels*, 196.

Page 98: "Every night she'd . . . about it": Norman, *We Band of Angels*, 187.

Page 99: "No, no, don't . . . him again": Frances Nash quoted in Williams, *To the Angels*, 163–164.

Page 99: "The Commander-in-Chief . . . the New Year": Nixon, *Delayed Manila*, 78.

Pages 100–101: "but it was impossible . . . and death": Nixon, *Delayed Manila*, 76.

Page 101: "I couldn't stand . . . in sheets": *Reminiscences of Two Former P.O.W. Army Nurses in World War II*, 13.

Page 101: "The people were . . . the bodies": Monahan, *All This Hell*, 152.

Page 101: "people would come . . . more food" and further Frances Nash quotes in Chapter 16: Norman, *We Band of Angels*, 199.

CHAPTER 17: LIBERATION!

Page 103: "Roll out . . . or tomorrow": Nixon, *Delayed Manila*, 83.

Page 104: "Hello, folks!": *The Santo Tomas Story*, 406.

Page 104: "Oh God, I was happy" and all Blaine quotes in Chapter 17: Norman, *We Band of Angels*, 206–210.

Page 105: "We had good army . . . the toilets": Cates, *The Drainpipe Diary*, 249.

Page 105: "It was too confusing . . . captivity routines": Williams, *To the Angels*, 216.

Page 106: Sallie Durrett conversation: Sallie Durrett Farmer, ANC interview, May 25, 1984, 22–23.

Page 106: "As the shells tore . . . to danger" and "We were stunned . . . to do their work": Cates, *The Drainpipe Diary*, 249–250.

Page 107: "Aren't you one . . . go home": Blaine conversation, Norman, *We Band of Angels*, 210.

Page 108: "We realized . . . they arrived": Monahan, *All This Hell*, 147.

Page 108: "Dear God . . . to say": *The Saga of Margaret Nash, WWII POW*, 12.

Page 109: "Do you have any food": Fessler, *No Time for Fear*, 99.

Page 109: "Run, run, run to the beach!": unidentified newspaper

clipping, WMSAMF, MFC, Margaret Alice Nash Collection, WWII, #2158.

Page 109: "We were lucky . . . with beriberi" and all Peggy Nash quotes in Chapter 17: *The Saga of Margaret Nash, WWII POW*, 14.

CHAPTER 18: HOMECOMING

Page 111: "I gained twenty pounds in twenty days": "Nurses Captured by Japanese Coming Home on Furlough," unidentified news clipping, WMSAMF, WMC, #1138.

Page 112: Lewey and Zwicker quotes: Norman, *We Band of Angels*, 224.

Page 112: "I'd had someone . . . I didn't know": Cindy Edwards, "WWII Nurse-POW from Jefferson Honored in Capital," *Marshall News Messenger*, Marshall, TX (April 8, 1983), 1A.

Page 112: "It all seemed . . . were living" and "This is the greatest . . . just numb": Norman, *We Band of Angels*, 224–225.

Page 113: "At dinner the other . . . next meal": Monahan, *All This Hell*, 73.

Page 114: "I was sure . . . our lives": Norman, *We Band of Angels*, 243.

Page 114: "We had a ball . . . gussied up": Palmer James, interview, 42.

Page 114: "the Army sent us . . . your family": Dalton Manning, author interview.

Page 115: "You had to sort . . . nervous wreck": Dworsky Henderson, interview, 29.

Page 115: "I began to feel . . . a freak": Fessler, *No Time for Fear*, 103.

Page 115: "They took X-ray . . . to live": *The Saga of Margaret Nash, WWII POW*, 17.

Pages 116: "What are all those people out there for?" and all further Peggy Nash quotes in Chapter 18: "V-J Day: County's Only Female POW Looks Back," *The Times Leader*, Wilkes-Barre, PA (August 14, 1985), 1.

CHAPTER 19: FORGOTTEN

Page 117: "They shared an incredible . . . them survive": Sandy Thor, author interview, November 8, 2011.

Page 117: "The trouble started . . . to him" and all Millie Dalton Manning quotes in Chapter 19: author interview.

Page 119: "My dear lieutenant! . . ." conversation: Danner, *What a Way to Spend a War*, 210.

Page 119: "But I wasn't able to . . . nobody was": Norman, *We Band of Angels*, 256.

Page 119: "chopped off my arms . . . me pregnant": Captain Rosemary Hogan, "What Did NOT Happen to the Bataan Nurses," *Liberty: The Magazine of a Free People* (November 17, 1945), 19, 80, 82.

Page 119: "Well, where's your baby?": WMFC, #11267.

Page 119: "What in the world . . . my face": Lieutenant Colonel Brantley, interview by Knox, 3.

Page 119: "Now you're going . . . a stigma": Monahan, *All This Hell*, 177.

Pages 119–120: "The mother of a . . . a breakdown": Lucy Wilson Jopling, *Warrior in White* (San Antonio, TX: The Water Cress Press, 1990), 62.

Page 120: "I have often wondered . . . to others": Norman, *We Band of Angels*, 242.

Page 120: "I came back . . . any children" and all Peggy Nash quotes in Chapter 19: *The Saga of Margaret Nash, WWII POW*, 19–19a.

Pages 120–121: "Well, sir, I can't . . . get about" Proceedings of Army Retiring Board for Officers, September 18, 1946, Serial number N-703470, First Lieutenant ANC Frankie T. Lewey, DOB 22 Nov 1910.

Page 121: "They'll take care . . . need them": Norman, *We Band of Angels*, 234.

Page 121: "prescription for endurance

and courage": Norman, *We Band of Angels*, 233.

Pages 121–122: "one of the . . . captivity warrant" and "They gave unstintingly . . . civilian internees . . .": Norman, *We Band of Angels*, 239.

Page 122: "No one ever gave . . ." and all Madeline M. Ullom quotes in Chapter 19: Transcript of testimony submitted to Senator Dennis DeConcini, member of the U.S. Senate Veterans Affairs Committee, Phoenix, AZ, January 26, 1982, courtesy American Defenders of Bataan & Corregidor, Inc.

Page 123: Letter to Ethel Thor from War Claims Commission July 21, 1953, courtesy Sandy Thor.

Page 123: "In 1978 . . . an evaluation": Sallie Durrett Farmer, ANC interview, May, 25, 1984, 17.

Page 123: "I had beriberi . . . of my skin": Dalton Manning author interview.

CHAPTER 20: MOVING ON

Page 124: "She was quiet . . . private person": Carla Kingsbury, author interview, September 3, 2011, Gig Harbor, WA.

Page 124: "In the camp that crusty . . . her again": Linda Bradley phone author interview, September 9, 2011.

Page 125: "I've never talked . . . here now": "Ex-POWs Evoke Memories: 'Angel of Bataan' Recalls Years in Internment Camp," *The Seattle Times*, Seattle, WA (March 11, 1991), E3.

Page 125: "Those eyes just followed us": Minnie Breese Stubbs, DOD interview, Bolling Air Force Base, Washington, D.C., April 9, 1983, 14.

Page 125: "Walking out in . . . my life": Jopling, *Warrior in White*, 42.

Page 125: "Being a 'senior' . . . in combat": Nesbit Davis to Starbuck, 1–2.

Page 125: "He still has horrible . . . and protector": Norman, *We Band of Angels*, 250.

Page 125: "My roommate . . . lives, practically": Dworsky Henderson, interview, 20.

Page 125: "To tell the truth . . . the baby": *The Saga of Margaret Nash, WWII POW*, 19.

Page 125: Elizabeth to Peggy Nash: July 31, 1989, courtesy of WMSAMF, WMC.

Page 126: "When I was in . . . the question" and all conversations with Susan Jerrett Trout and Frankie Lewey in Chapter 20: Author interview.

Page 127: "I must have been . . . my nightgown" and "I never cried. . . . do that": Norman, *We Band of Angels*, 244.

Page 127: "She was one tough lady . . . United Nations": All quotes from George V. (Van) Millett III, author phone interview, February 2, 2012.

Page 128: "I never made it . . . full life": Thomas, Loydean, "Internal Defenses: Former Nurse and Prisoner of War Recalls How She Survived Captivity with Pride and Ingenuity," *San Antonio Express-News* (February 1, 1991), 3.

Page 128: "She was a remarkably . . . Purple Heart": Kathi Mullin, author interview, March 20, 2012.

Page 128: "then they realized . . . who I was": Brantley, WMC interview.

Page 128: "It's a full-time job, but it's kind of fun": Brantley, WMC interview.

Page 130: "I was stunned . . . on Corregidor" and all Carolyn Torrence quotes in Chapter 20: Author phone interview, September 9, 2011.

Page 130: "Going to Santo Tomas . . . their memories": Bradley, interview.

Page 130: "I wouldn't want . . . learn from it": Author interview with Carolyn Torrence.

Page 130: "I believe the . . . to endure": Bartimus, Tad, "Angel of Bataan

Returns to Manila," *St. Louis Post-Dispatch* (December 14, 1980), 3F.

CHAPTER 21: RECOGNITION AT LAST

Page 133: "She had the sweetest . . . more pronounced": Susan Sacharski, Northwestern Memorial Hospital Archivist, author phone interview, September 27, 2011.

Page 133: "I cut clothes off . . . a blister" and all Dalton Manning quotes in Chapter 21: Author interview.

BIBLIOGRAPHY

An asterisk (*) indicates books suitable for young readers.

"Angels of Bataan Saved—Work On!" *San Francisco News*, February 5, 1945.

Army Nurse Corps Oral History Program interview, Department of the Army, Center for Military History, Washington, D.C.—Adams, Phyllis Arnold; Chambers, Beatrice E.; Farmer, Sallie Durrett; Haynes, Edith Shacklette; James, Rita Palmer; Lloyd, Edith Corns; Terrill, Dorothy Still; Moore, Inez McDonald. Army Medical Department Center of History and Heritage (AMEDD), Fort Sam Houston, TX.

Bartimus, Tad, "Angel of Bataan Returns to Manila." *St. Louis Post-Dispatch*, December 14, 1980, 3F.

Bartsch, William H. *I Wonder at Times How We Keep Going Here: The 1941–42 Philippines Diary of Lt. John P. Burns, 21st Pursuit Squadron.* www.highbeam.com/doc/1G1-157097840.html, accessed April 4, 2013.

"Bataan Nurse Describes Hospital No. 2 Drama." *Post News Magazine*, Fort Sam Houston, TX, 1992.

Bernatitus, Ann, NC, USN, (Ret.). Oral history dated January 25, 1994, provided courtesy of the Historian, Bureau of Medicine and Surgery. http://www.history.navy.mil/faqs/faq87-3b.htm, accessed February 22, 2013.

Bisceglia, Michael. "Just A Girl From Hampton: 1st. Lt. Rita G. (Palmer) James." *Hampton Union*, Friday, Hampton, NJ, October 26, 2007. http://www.hampton.lib.nh.us/hampton/biog/ritapalmer/ritapalmerfromhamtonHU20071026.htm, accessed January 28, 2013.

Bradley, Linda. Phone author interview, September 9, 2011.

Butler, Allen, Julian Ruffin, Marion Sniffen et al. "The Nutritional Status of Civilians Rescued from Japanese Prison Camps." *New England Journal of Medicine* 233 (November 29, 1945): 639–52.

*Cates, Tressa R., R.N. *The Drainpipe Diary*. New York: Vantage Press, 1957.

Coville, Cabot. "Our Two Months on Corregidor." *The Saturday Evening Post* (June 27, 1942), 15, 100,102.

Danner, Dorothy Still. *What a Way to Spend a War: Navy Nurse POWs in the Philippines*. Annapolis, MD: Naval Institute Press, 1995.

Department of Defense Interviews, Washington, D.C., April 9, 1983. Brantley, Lieutenant Colonel Hattie R.; Clark, Anna Eleanor Williams; Mealor, Gladys Ann; Henderson, Bertha Dworsky; Hively, Verna; Jenkins, Geneva; Nesbit, Major (Ret.) Josephine; Stubbs, Minnie Breese; Ullom, Lieutenant Colonel (Ret.) Madeline.

Duckworth, James. *Official History of General Hospital #1 USAFFE at Camp Limay Bataan: Little Baguio, Camp O'Donnell, Tarlac, Philippine Islands, from Dec. 23, 1941, to June 30, 1942*. National Archives, Philippine Archives Collection, Washington, D.C., Record Group 407, Box 12.

Dyess, Lieutenant Colonel William E. *Bataan Death March: A Survivor's Account*. Lincoln: University of Nebraska Press, 2002.

Edwards, Cindy. "WWII Nurse-POW from Jefferson Honored in Capital." *Marshall News Messenger*, Marshall, TX, April 8, 1983.

*Fessler, Diane Burke. *No Time for Fear: Voices of American Military Nurses in World War II*. East Lansing: Michigan State University Press, 1996.

Geister, J. "Nurses Stood By to the End." *Trained Nurse and Hospital Review*, 198, 343–46, New York, 1942.

Glusman, John A. *Conduct Under Fire: Four American Doctors and Their Fight for Life as Prisoners of the Japanese, 1941–1945*. New York: Viking, 2005.

Hartendorf, A. V. *The Santo Tomas Story, Edited from the Official History of the Santo Tomas Internment Camp by F. H. Golay*. New York: McGraw-Hill, 1964.

Hayes, Ada N. "Three Years in a Prison Camp." *Hampton Union*, May 10, 1945. http://www.hampton.lib.nh.us/hampton/biog/ritapalmer/3yearsinaprisoncamp.htm, accessed February 11, 2013.

Hogan, Captain Rosemary. "What Did *Not* Happen to the Bataan Nurses." *Liberty: The Magazine of a Free People* (November 17, 1945), 19, 80, 82.

Imparato, Edward T. *General MacArthur Speeches & Reports: 1908–1964*. New York: Turner Publishing Company, 2000.

Jopling, Lucy Wilson. *Warrior in White*. San Antonio, TX: The Water Cress Press, 1990.

Kaminski, Theresa. *Prisoners in Paradise: American Women in the Wartime South Pacific*. Lawrence: University Press of Kansas, 2000.

Keith, Lawrence. "An 'Angel of Bataan.'"

Owensboro Message-Inquirer, Owensboro, Kentucky, December 26, 1994, 2A. WMFC, #1357.

Kingsbury, Carla. Author interview, September 3, 2011, Gig Harbor, WA.

Knox, Warren. Interview with Lieutenant Colonel Hattie Brantley, Retired Army Nurse Corps Association Convention, April 28, 1980, San Antonio, TX.

*Kuhn, Betsy. *Angels of Mercy, The Army Nurses of World War II.* New York: Atheneum Books for Young Readers, 1999.

Leovy, Jill. "Ex-POWs Evoke Memories: 'Angel of Bataan' Recalls Years in Internment Camp." *The Seattle Times*, Seattle, WA, March 11, 1991. http://community.seattle times.nwsource.com/archive/? date=19910311&slug=1271082, accessed February 21, 2013.

Letter from Josephine Nesbit Davis, Major ANC, to Dorothy L. Starbuck, Chief Benefits Director, Veterans Administration, January 15, 1983, 2, courtesy American Defenders of Bataan & Corregidor, Inc.

Letter to Ethel Thor from War Claims Commission, July 21, 1953, courtesy Sandy Thor.

Letter to Vivian Johnson from Corregidor evacuee Susan Downing Gallagher, June 13, 1943, courtesy Sandy Thor.

"Liberated Jap Prisoners Hold Reunion." *Vidette-Messenger*, Valparaiso, IN, March 3, 1945, 1.

Manning, Mildred (Millie) Dalton. Author interview, January 29, 2012, Trenton, NJ.

Manning, Mildred (Millie) Dalton. Women in Military Service to America Foundation, Inc. Women's Memorial Foundation Collection. Interview, January 29, 2008.

Marechal-Workman, Andree. Oakland

Naval Hospital Public Affairs (ONHPA). Interview transcript, Oakland, CA, September 10, 1992.

Martin, J. C. "A Christmas Present Nurse Will Never Forget." *The Arizona Daily Star*, Tuscon, AZ. December 25, 1977. WMSAMF, Madeline M. Ullom Collection, #2118.

Millett, George V. (Van) III. Author phone interview, February 2, 2012.

Monahan, Evelyn M. and Rosemary Neidel-Greenlee. *All This Hell: U.S. Nurses Imprisoned by the Japanese.* Lexington: The University Press of Kentucky, 2000.

Monahan, Evelyn M. and Rosemary Neidel-Greenlee. *And If I Perish: Frontline U.S. Army Nurses in World War II.* New York: Anchor Books, 2004.

Mooney, Tom. "V-J Day: County's Only Female POW Looks Back." *The Times Leader*, Wilkes-Barre, PA, August 14, 1985.

Morton, Louis. *The War in the Pacific: The Fall of the Philippines.* Washington, D.C.: Center for Military History, Government Printing Office, 1953.

Nash, Margaret. *The Saga of Margaret Nash, WWII POW.* Transcription of interview, Women in Military Service to America Memorial Foundation, Inc., Women's Memorial Collection, Arlington, VA.

Nesbit, Josephine. *History of the Army Nurse Corps in the Philippine Islands, September 1949–February 1945.* Unpublished manuscript (AMEDD).

Nixon, Eva Anna. *Delayed Manila.* Newberg, OR: Friendsview Manor, 1981.

Norman, Elizabeth M. *We Band of Angels: The Untold Story of American Nurses Trapped on Bataan by the Japanese.* New York: Pocket Books, 1999.

"Nurses Captured by Japanese Coming

Home on Furlough," unidentified newsclipping, WMSAMF, WMC, #1138.

Proceedings of Army Retiring Board for Officers. September 18, 1946, Serial number N-703470, First Lieutenant ANC Frankie T. Lewey, DOB November 22, 1910.

Redmond, Juanita. *I Served on Bataan.* Philadelphia: L.B. Lippincott Company, 1943.

Reminiscences of Two Former P.O.W. Army Nurses in World War I. Transcript of taped interview, WMFC, #1875, March 2, 1983.

Rogers, Mary. "A Prisoner of War Remembers." *The Beaver County Times*, Beaver, PA, May 3, 2003, B7. http://news.google.com/ newspapers?nid=2002& dat=20030504&id=sBovAAAA IBAJ&sjid=ZtsFAAAAIBA J&pg=1819,672069, accessed February 10, 2013.

Roosevelt, Franklin D. Address to the People of the Philippines on Post-War Independence, August 12, 1943. http://www.presidency.ucsb.edu/ ws/?pid=16443#axzz1iWEsQQif, accessed February 19, 2013.

Russell, Maxine K., ed. *Jungle Angel: Bataan Remembered: The Testimony of Hortense E. McKay to Maxine K. Russell.* Brainerd, MN: Bang Printing Company, 1988.

Sacharski, Susan. Northwestern Memorial Hospital Archivist. Author phone interview. September 27, 2011.

Schaefer, Chris. *Bataan Diary: An American Family in World War II 1941–1945.* Houston, TX: Riverview Publishing, 2004.

Sears, Barbara. *Tucsonan Will Observe Corregidor Anniversary.* WMSAMF, Madeline Ullom Collection #2118.

"Sharp Skirmishes in The Philippines Seen As Opening of Japanese Drive."

New York Times, March 22, 1942, 1A.

Stevens, F. H. *Santo Tomas Prison Internment Camp*. New York: Stratford House, 1946.

Thomas, Loydean. "Internal Defenses: Former Nurse and Prisoner of War Recalls How She Survived Captivity with Pride and Ingenuity." *San Antonio Express-News*, February 1, 1991, 3.

Thor, Ethel, letters home. Courtesy Sandy Thor, Seattle, WA.

*Tomblin, Barbara Brooks. *GI Nightingales: Army Nurses in WWII*. Lexington: University Press of Kentucky, 2003.

Torrence, Carolyn A. Author phone interview, September 9, 2011.

Trout, Susan Jerrett. Author interviews, Kirkland, WA, September 7, 2010, November 11, 2011, April 15, 2012.

U.S. War Department letter. Courtesy Sandy Thor.

Ullom, Madeline M. ANC (Ret.). Transcript of testimony submitted to Senator Dennis DeConcini, Member of the U.S. Senate Veterans Affairs Committee, Phoenix, AZ, January 26, 1982, courtesy American Defenders of Bataan & Corregidor, Inc.

Unit History and personal roster of General Hospital No. 2, December 41 to June 42. Author and date unknown. Washington, D.C.: National Archives, Philippine Archive Collection.

Wainwright, Jonathan M. and Robert Considine, ed. *General Wainwright's Story: The Account of Four Years of Humiliating Defeat, Surrender, and Captivity*. New York: Doubleday & Company, 1946.

Weinstein, Alfred A., M.D. *Barbed-Wire Surgeon*. New York: The Macmillan Company, 1950.

Weinzheimer, Sascha. Author phone interview, August 21, 2012.

*Williams, Denny. *To the Angels*. San Francisco: Denson Press, 1985.

Zwicker, Alice. Diary. Courtesy Rod Tenny.

WEB SITES FOR MORE INFORMATION

American Defenders of Bataan & Corregidor, Inc., philippine-defenders.lib.wv.us/

Bellafaire, Judith L. *The Army Nurse Corps: A Commemoration of World War II Service*, www.history.army.mil/catalog/pubs/72/72-14.html

Corregidor Historic Society, The: Corregidor Then and Now, corregidor.org/_admin/CTN_central/ctn_ghq_index_composite.htm

Official Gazette of the Office of the President of the Philippines, www.gov.ph/featured/world-war-ii-in-the-philippines/

Report on American Prisoners of War Interned by the Japanese in the Philippine Islands, Prepared by Office of the Provost Marshal General, November 19, 1945, www.mansell.com/pow_resources/camplists/philippines/pows_in_pi-OPMG_report.html

National Women's History Museum, www.nwhm.org/online-exhibits/partners/4.htm

U.S. Army in World War II series, www.history.army.mil/html/bookshelves/collect/usaww2.html

Women in Military Service for America Memorial Foundation, www.womensmemorial.org/

World War II Database, ww2db.com/photo.php?source=all&color=all&list=search&foreigntype=B&foreigntype_id=46

Young, Al, *My Father's Captivity*, www.alyoung.com/My_Fathers_Captivity/

ACKNOWLEDGMENTS

THEY SAY IT TAKES A VILLAGE TO RAISE A child. It certainly took one to create this book. From the very first idea to the last comma, not one bit could I have done alone. I offer my deep gratitude to everyone who gave of themselves to help bring *Pure Grit* to fruition. The journey has taught me much about courage, perseverance, generosity, and grace.

Any errors of research are completely mine, and not due to any of those who so generously aided me. After living with the stories of the POW nurses for nearly five years, I feel as if I know these women. I am especially grateful to those who helped me come to know them and their experiences so well. I am greatly in debt to Elizabeth Norman, Evelyn M. Monahan, and Rosemary Neidel-Greenlee, whose conscientious, groundbreaking research and passionate, skillful writing first opened my heart to these women. To Mildred Dalton Manning for kindly allowing me an interview, to her son James Manning, and to all the family members of nurses who so generously shared their memories, photographs, personal mementos, and documents: Susan Jerrett Trout, Linda Bradley, Carla Kingsbury, Sandy Thor, Carolyn Armold Torrence, Kathi Mullin, Ric James, Barbara Wagar, Dr. George V. Millett III and his wife Ann Millet, Susan Johnson, Dana Difford, Rod Tenny, Dennis Kennedy, Stanford Brantley and Kenneth Brantley; also Sascha Weinzheimer, a Santo Tomas internee; and Anne Fadiman, whose mother, Annalee Jacoby, was a journalist on Bataan who photographed the nurses and escaped before the surrender.

Others who were very helpful to my research: Robbie Fee, director, Oral History Program, Women in Military Service for America Memorial Foundation; Britta Granrud, curator of collections, Women's Memorial Foundation; Lieutenant Colonel Nancy B. Cantrell, Army Nurse Corps historian; and Mary Hope, senior archivist at AMEDD Center of History and Heritage; Gary Trogdon and Michael Yarborough, U.S. Army Center of Military History; James Tobias, Historical Resources Branch, U.S. Army Center of Military History; Luther Hanson, Ft. Lee Quartermaster Museum; James W. Zobel, MacArthur Memorial Museum; Paul Theerman, Images and Archives Section, History of Medicine Division, National Library of Medicine; Michael Rhode and André B. Sobocinski,

U.S. Navy Bureau of Medicine and Surgery, Office of Medical History.

Holly Reed, archives specialist, Still Pictures Reference, National Archives; Susan Sacharski, archivist, Northwestern Memorial Hospital; Bill Teschek, Lane Memorial Library; Mike Lebens, curator of collections, The National Museum of the Pacific War, James Bowen Pacific War Historical Society, Spokane Public Library; Lucille Kirkeby, museum researcher, Crow Wing County Historical Society.

From American Defenders of Bataan & Corregidor: Caroline Burkhart, vice president; George Wallace, editor, *The Quan*; Cheryl Cerbone, editor, American Ex-Prisoners of War Bulletin; and Linda Dahl, POW history project manager.

Thanks to historians Diane Fessler and William Harry Boudreau; Paul Whitman, Corrigedor.proboards.com; and Mike Falkenstein.

John Gobbell, for details on WWII aircraft; Don McPherson, F6F-5 Hellcat pilot; Lee Hanna on Goodreads.

For particular help with images, John Tewell, Al Young, and Jan Thompson.

For sparking the idea for this book, Joyce Engels.

With great appreciation to my agent, Stephen Fraser, who found a wonderful home for this book at Abrams. And to all the folks at Abrams who took my vision, believed in it, cleaned it up, and made it real and beautiful and powerful—thank you! To my editor Howard Reeves, editorial assistant Melissa Faulner, managing editor Jen Graham, and designer Maria Middleton, I so appreciate your talents and hard work and am so fortunate to work with you.

Wholehearted gratitude to my writing group—Beth Cooley, Kris Dinnison, Mary Douthitt, Claire Rudolf Murphy, and Meghan Nuttall Sayers. I would not be the writer I am without you.

To my friends and family, who are there for me every day and support me in my writing—I cannot thank you enough. You know who you are and how much I love and value you. Love and thanks to Brandon, Monica, and Dylan, who may have gotten short shrift due to Mom's obsession with writing. Michael, my love, thank you for your generous support, both emotionally and financially. You're my favorite.

IMAGE CREDITS

Page 10: Courtesy Sandra Thor. **Page 11:** U.S. Army Medical Department. **Page 12:** Courtesy Sandra Thor. **Page 13:** Time & Life Pictures/Getty Images. **Page 14:** Courtesy Floramund F. Difford/Lt. Col. Dana Difford. **Page 15, top:** US Navy Office of Medical History. **Page 15, bottom:** Women in Military Service for America Memorial Foundation, Inc. **Page 16:** Courtesy Floramund F. Difford/Lt. Col. Dana Difford. **Page 17:** National Archives and Records. **Page 18:** Courtesy Floramund F. Difford/Lt. Col. Dana Difford. **Page 19:** U.S. Naval Historical Foundation. **Page 20:** Courtesy Al Young Studios. **Page 21:** Courtesy Floramund F. Difford. **Page 22:** Courtesy Sandra Thor. **Page 23:** Courtesy U.S. Army Center for Military History. **Page 24:** Courtesy Sandra Thor. **Page 25:** U.S. Naval Historical Foundation. **Page 26:** © CriticalPast.com. **Page 28:** Women in Military Service Memorial Photo Collection. **Page 29, top:** National Archives and Records. **Page 29, bottom:** Courtesy Susan Jerrett Trout. **Page 30:** Courtesy Sandra Thor. **Page 31:** With permission of Anne Fadiman and the Estate of Annalee Whitmore Jacoby Fadiman. Images © Melville Jacoby. Used with permission. All rights reserved. **Page 33:** Courtesy Susan Jerrett Trout. **Page 34:** Author's collection. **Page 35, top and bottom:** National Archives and Records. **Pages 36–37:** U.S. Center for Military History. **Page 38:** With permission of Anne Fadiman and the Estate of Annalee Whitmore Jacoby Fadiman. Images © Melville Jacoby. Used with permission. All rights reserved. **Page 39, top:** Courtesy Georege V. Millett III. **Page 39, bottom:** National Archives and Records. **Page 41:** Associated Press. **Page 42:** Dorothy Scholl Armold Papers. **Pages 43–45:** With permission of Anne Fadiman and the Estate of Annalee Whitmore Jacoby Fadiman. Images © Melville Jacoby. Used with permission. All rights reserved. **Page 46:** American Defenders of Bataan and Corregidor. **Page 47:** Courtesy Sandra Thor. **Page 48:** Rita Palmer James Documents. **Page 49:** Courtesy Elizabeth Norman. **Page 50:** Courtesy Sally Blaine/Elizabeth Norman. **Page 51:** © CriticalPast.com. **Page 53:** With permission of Anne Fadiman and the Estate of Annalee Whitmore Jacoby Fadiman. Images © Melville Jacoby. Used with permission. All rights reserved. **Page 54:** Courtesy Susan Jerrett Trout. **Page 56:** Courtesy Jan Thompson. **Page 57:** Getty Images, Hulton Archive. **Pages 58–59:** National Archives and Records. **Page 60:** © CriticalPast.com. **Pages 61–62:** National Archives and Records. **Page 63:** Courtesy USS Gold Star. **Page 66:** U.S. Naval Historical Foundation. **Page 67, top:** General Douglas MacArthur Foundation. **Page 67, bottom:** © CriticalPast.com. **Page 68:** Getty Images, Hulton Archive. **Page 69:** U.S. Army Medical Museum. **Page 70:** Dorothy Scholl Armold Papers. **Page 72:** Popperfoto/Getty Images. **Page 73:** National Archives and Records. **Page 74:** Women in Military Serivce for America Memorial Foundation, Inc. **Page 75:** Author's collection. **Page 76:** General Douglas MacArthur Foundation. **Page 77:** Time & Life Pictures/Getty Images. **Page 78:** Women in Military Servrce for America Memorial Foundation, Inc. **Page 80:** National Archives and Records. **Page 81:** Courtesy Sandra Thor. **Page 82:** National Archives and Records. **Page 83:** Courtesy of the American Red Cross. All rights reserved in all countries. **Page 84:** Time & Life Pictures/Getty Images. **Page 85:** Courtesy Sandra Thor. **Page 87:** National Archives and Records. **Page 88:** Time & Life Pictures/Getty Images. **Page 92:** Courtesy of the Family of Warren R. Stewart, Jr. **Page 93:** National Archives and Records/Courtesy John Tewell. **Page 94:** Time & Life Pictures/Getty Images. **Page 95:** General Douglas MacArthur Foundation. **Page 97:** Time & Life Pictures/Getty Images. **Page 98:** National Archives and Records. **Pages 99–100:** National Archives and Records/John Tewell. **Page 102:** National Archives and Records. **Page 103:** Time & Life Pictures/Getty Images. **Page 105:** National Archives and Records. **Page 106–107:** Courtesy John Tewell. **Page 109:** Associated Press Photo/U.S. Army Signal Corps. **Page 110:** Time Life Pictures/Getty Images. **Page 111:** U.S. Army Center for Military History. **Page 112:** U.S. Army Center for Military History. **Page 113:** Dorothy Scholl Armold Papers. **Page 114, top:** Courtesy George V. Millett III. **Page 114, bottom and 115:** U.S. Navy Bureau of Medicine, Office of Medical History. **Page 116:** Author's collection. **Page 117:** Baylor Health Care System. **Page 118, top left:** Rita Palmer James Documents. **Page 118, right:** Liberty Magazine/Rod Tenny. **Page 122:** Women in Military Service for America Memorial Foundation, Inc. **Page 124:** Courtesy Sandra Thor. **Page 126:** Courtesy Susan Jerrett Trout. **Page 127:** George V. Millett III. **Page 129–130:** Courtesy Floramund Fellmeth Difford/Lt. Col. Dana Difford. **Page 131:** Women in Military Serivce for America Memorial Foundation, Inc. **Page 132, left:** Dorothy Scholl Armold Papers. **Page 132, right:** © Stevenson Que.

INDEX